FROM DARKNESS INTO LIGHT

The first women students admitted to Tehran University in September 1936. Mrs. Bámdád is third from the right in the front row.

FROM DARKNESS INTO LIGHT:
WOMEN'S EMANCIPATION IN IRAN

by
Badr ol-Moluk Bámdád

*Edited and
Translated by*
F. R. C. Bagley

AN EXPOSITION-UNIVERSITY BOOK

Exposition Press   Hicksville, New York

HQ
1768
.B 3513

FIRST EDITION

© 1977 by F. R. C. Bagley

Copyright © under the Universal Copyright
and Bern Conventions

All rights reserved, including the right of reproduction in whole or in part, in any form or by any means, electronic or mechanical, including photocopying, recording, or by any information storage and retrieval system, without permission in writing from the Publisher. Inquiries should be addressed to Exposition Press, Inc., 900 South Oyster Bay Road, Hicksville, N.Y. 11801.

Library of Congress Catalog Card Number: 76-50308

ISBN 0-682-48705-8

Printed in the United States of America

CONTENTS

ACKNOWLEDGMENT ix
TRANSLATOR'S PREFACE xi
A NOTE ON THE AUTHORESS xvii
by Mrs. Shams ol-Moluk Javáher-e Kalám

I. EQUALITY OF RIGHTS—A Long-Standing Human Aspiration 3

II. IRANIAN WOMEN IN BYGONE DAYS 7
The centuries of darkness. The first signs of women's awakening. Marriage and the veil. Men's apartments and women's apartments. Contracts with the outside world through "brokeresses." A favorite meeting place for women—the Turkish bath. "Wish-blouses." Absurd restrictions on women. Women one side, men the other. How Iranian children shared their mothers' miseries. Tutors and Qor'án schools. Religious instruction in the harem. Not addressing women by their real names.

III. THE CONSTITUTIONAL REVOLUTION (1906-1911) AND WOMEN'S AWAKENING 25
Women's efforts and setbacks. The Women's Freedom Society. A constitutionalist princess in a secret society. Náser ol-Din Sháh's liberal-minded, favorite daughter. The first public demonstration by women. The unknown woman soldier. The first girls' schools. A resolute pioneer. A mojtahed's wife who founded

a girls' school. Another devoutly religious pioneer. The Tarbiat Girls' School and the constitutionalist lady who founded it. The opinion of a pioneer. The role of the American Girls' School. The Ecole Franco-Persane.

IV. AFTER THE FIRST WORLD WAR   55
The reunification and modernization of Iran under Rezá Sháh the Great. The tragedy of a headmistress and artist. The first official help for girls' education. The Women's Teacher Training College. Self-defense by college girls. Steps to improve midwifery. Mohtaram Eskandari and the foundation of the Patriotic Women's League. The league's second president. The league's secretary and adult-class organizer; its first theatrical show. The first teacher of the adult class. Another member who was a teacher, journalist and poetess. "A Woman's Beauty." The weapon of the pen. "Homá Mahmudi's Reply to F. Barzgar" (in the newspaper Irán, *1923). "A Poem by Homá Mahmudi" (in the periodical* Álam-e Nesván, *1922). "A Poem by Homá Mahmudi in Reply to Criticism by Mrs. Senowbar Atábekián" (in* Álam-e Nesván, *1922). Banished for the cause. One way of making the women's feelings known. The first women's international congress in Iran. A constructive rebel. The first unveiled Iranian woman teacher. The clash of old and new ideas. Girls' education in the provinces. An unsuccessful experiment. The theater in the cause of women's uplift. Ali Akbar Siási's play* Máh-Pár *and the actress Varto Tarián.*

V. THE DAYBREAK   91
The reforms of Rezá Sháh the Great. The formation of the Ladies' Center. A momentous decree. The

Contents

       top pupils of the year 1935. Women gain access to higher education. The first woman university lecturer. The first woman professor. The first woman lawyer. A great poetess.

VI. TROUBLED TIMES   105
       Effects of the Second World War. An upsurge of reaction. The women's response. The first federative body. The founder of the Council of Women. The founder of the New Path Society. A life given to social service. An exponent of women's rights in Islam. The High Council of Iranian Women's Associations.

VII. THE WINNING OF EQUAL RIGHTS   115
       The White Revolution. Women and municipal councils. Women and the referendum. A demonstration outside the senate. Women's gratitude and loyalty to the Sháhansháh. The charter of equal citizenship. Women in parliament and in elected councils. A new campaign against women's illiteracy. The future of the women's movement. The Family Protection Law. A triumph for Iranian women. The Women's Literacy Corps. New horizons of work and service. International appreciation of the Iranian women's movement. The task ahead.

APPENDICES

A. *Some poems.*   133
"Women in Iran," Parvin E'tesámi (1906-1941). "Women in Shrouds," Mirzázádeh Eshqi (1893-1924). "No More Veils Like These," Malek ol-Sho'ará Bahár (1886-1950). "Ruffled Locks," Áref Qazvini (1882-1934). "The Hypocrisy," Iraj Mirzá Jalál ol-Mamálek.

B. *Publications edited by women (1909-1969).*   139

ACKNOWLEDGMENT

Gratitude is due to
MRS. ELIZABETH HOLLOWS
*for secretarial help
in the making of this translation*

TRANSLATOR'S PREFACE

The lively discussions of women's rights in recent years have coincided with a growth of American and European interest in one of the world's oldest civilized countries, Iran. A sketch of the Iranian women's movement may therefore be useful to not only people who have contacts with Iran but also to a wider readership. The present work has been translated from two Persian books by one of the movement's most energetic leaders, Mrs. Badr ol-Moluk Bámdád. Its appearance at this time is appropriate because 1975 was International Women's Year and 1976 marks the start of the second half-century of the Pahlavi dynasty, whose two Shahs are regarded by Iranian women as their liberators.

The foreigner visiting Iran today meets Iranian women as a matter of course at places of work and in hospitable Iranian homes. Seventy or even fifty years ago, he seldom if ever met any Iranian women at all, and only knew that the walking black bundles which he saw in the street were women because he was told so. The revolution in the position of women is perhaps the most fundamental of the many great changes which have taken place in Iran since the start of the struggle for constitutional government in 1906 and the accession of the Pahlavi dynasty in 1925. It has enabled Iranian women to make fuller use of their energies and talents; it has made family life happier for wives and children and also for husbands; and it has helped mothers to bring up children in healthier and more mentally stimulating ways. These factors have made at least as great a contribution as other important factors, such as oil wealth and wise government, to Iran's present impressive national upsurge.

In general, women's emancipation is a modern phenomenon, linked to the growth of an urbanized and industrialized type of society. In mainly agricultural and pastoral societies, exposed to natural hazards and to frequent insecurity and warfare, the extended family or clan or tribe gave protection to mothers and children but offered women little scope for fulfillment except in the maternal and domestic roles. In Western Europe girls did not have much opportunity for education, and married women did not acquire legal responsibility and rights to own and manage property until the nineteenth century; and only in the twentieth century have women acquired the right to vote and other civic rights. On the other hand, in Europe women were not veiled or secluded, and individual women were sometimes able to attain high positions.

This is not the place to ask how and why in Iran and other Moslem countries it became customary until within living memory to veil and seclude women, and with rare exceptions to deny them education and to debar them from public life. The question is complex and has been discussed in many books. One of the best studies is in chapter two of R. Levy's book *The Social Structure of Islam* (Cambridge 1955), where references to all the relevant Qor'ánic verses are given. Suffice it to say that the sacred book of Islam puts women on an equal footing with men as believers and worshippers and in responsibility to God and hope of salvation. It allows women to acquire property by inheritance or earning and to manage it independently. While permitting marriage to as many as four wives and also temporary marriage, it clearly envisages such arrangements as necessary only in special circumstances and as not normally appropriate for the free man and the free woman. It permits but reprehends divorce, requires the husband to pause and reflect twice before deciding to divorce, and imposes a duty of effort to bring about reconciliation. It enjoins modesty in dress and deportment on women and also on men, but does not speak of seclusion. Women pilgrims have never been segregated from men in the performance of the annual ceremonies of the pilgrimage *(hajj)* at Mecca; and the pilgrim's garment *(ehrám)* does not cover the eyes and face. History shows that in the early days of Islam women played active parts in public life.

Translator's Preface

Likewise, in ancient Iran, women had an honorable status. In the sagas and romances of Ferdowsi's *Sháhnámeh (Book of Kings)*, which like other folklore probably embody a substratum of fact, the heroines are nearly always strong and good, while among the men there are weak kings as well as strong kings and villains as well as champions. In A.D. 630-631 two queens came to the Iranian throne, and one of them, Purándokht, is mentioned as an effective ruler, but she died after a few months.

It seems that the fashion of veiling and the harem arose in the caliphal court in the ninth century A.D. and spread downward through urban society, though not to peasants and nomads. The basic law books, written at that time and reflecting the then prevalent mood, generally stretch points to women's disadvantage. They treat polygamy and temporary marriage as normal, permit divorce after pronouncement of a formula three times without pause, and do not insist on the duty of effort to bring about reconciliation. In any case, seclusion and denial of education prevented women from making full use of their Qor'ánic rights. The general view came to be that women are "weak" not only in body but also in mind. An Arabic saying that "they (feminine) lack rationality" was often quoted, and attributed by some to the second caliph Omar. Education for women was therefore considered useless or even dangerous.

Even so, there were women who earned renown. Rábe'eh ol-Adavieh of Basra (d. 801) became one of Islam's most revered saints. History tells us of three reigning Moslem queens (Razieh Begom of Delhi, 1236-1240; Shajar ol-Dorr of Egypt, 1250-1257; Ábesh Khátun of Sbiráz, 1267-1284), and of influential royal ladies at various places and times. An eleventh-century Iranian poetess, Mahsati, is also remembered. It must be admitted, however, that such instances were rare.

From the late nineteenth century onward, thoughtful Iranians began to perceive that drastic political and social reforms were needed to avert the threats of internal decay and foreign domination, and some of them saw the fundamental importance of reforming the social and educational status of the women. Iranian women have never lacked patriotism, and some of them likewise began to revolt against the terrible frustration imposed by the harem and the veil. Although the most influential leaders of the reform movement were enlightened members of the Shi'ite Moslem clergy, most of the clergy and the majority of public opinion at the time still held traditional attitudes to women.

In these circumstances, the task of Iran's pioneer feminists was educational: to educate Iranian women for a fuller role by founding and running schools and to educate public opinion through the press. It was a long and hard task. Probably public opinion was not ready when Rezá Sháh took the bull by the horns and decreed the unveiling of Iranian women on 7 January 1936, and there was still a good deal of opposition in 1963 when Iranian women gained the right to vote and hold civic office as part of the White Revolution of Shah and People.

Mrs. Badr ol-Moluk Bámdád has devoted her abundant energies to both teaching and journalism, as well as work for women's organizations. A sketch of her career, written by her colleague and close friend Mrs. Shams ol-Moluk Javáher-e Kalám, appears at the end of this preface. Two episodes are particularly memorable. In 1923, Mrs. Bámdád, then aged eighteen, composed a book on domestic science (based partly on French works and partly on her own observations), which was the first Persian school textbook ever written by a woman, and for that very reason she had difficulty in getting it published. Eventually, it was printed in 1925 by order of Rezá Khán (then prime minister and war minister, soon to become Rezá Sháh) after the indomitable young authoress had managed to get a petition delivered to him. The book has been reprinted forty-eight times. In 1936 she was one of the first twelve women entrants to the University of Tehran (which had been constituted in 1934). Although the university regulations said nothing about men and women, the university authorities had presumed that women were ineligible, and it was only after Rezá Sháh had made his wishes known that these twelve qualified applicants were admitted.

As president of the Women's League of Supporters of the Universal Declaration of Human Rights, Mrs. Bámdád has worked

Translator's Preface

for fulfillment of the provisions of this declaration (issued by the U.N.O. on 10 December 1948) with respect to the women of Iran. The efforts of the Women's League have been rewarded by the important successes which are described in this book, and which owe so much to the firm resolve of H.I.M. the Sháhansháh to place Iran in the vanguard of modern progress and in particular to complete the emancipation of Iranian women begun by his father.

Mrs. Bámdád wrote the first volume of *Iranian Women from the Constitutional Revolution to the White Revolution* at the request of the league's members. It was published in Tehran in 1968. Its descriptions of present achievements and past conditions, and its accounts of the struggles and ordeals of the pioneers, aroused such interest among both older and younger readers that she was asked to write a supplement. Drawing on her own ample stock of memories, and using further information given by her many friends, she then wrote the second volume, which was published in Tehran in 1969.

In the present translation, the original texts have been faithfully rendered, but in view of the need to combine the two volumes into one, the order of the materials has been rearranged chronologically; as a help to readers not well acquainted with Iranian history and institutions and customs, brief explanations have been inserted either in the text or in footnotes. Some additions have also been made after consultation with the authoress.

Mrs. Bámdád's warmth of personality is matched by her delightful sense of humor, which is reflected in the book's many amusing passages. Above all, the book vividly depicts a past scene which existed within living memory but is rapidly being forgotten. Young Iranian women and men have no idea of the way in which their mothers and grandmothers had to live, or of the obstacles which the pioneers had to face. The ever more numerous foreigners who now visit Iran similarly take the competence and dignity of the country's women for granted. As readers will learn from this book, these were things which had to be fought for.

Mrs. Bámdád apologizes to readers for the book's inadequacy

as a history of Iranian feminism in the period 1906-1967. Besides the persons whom she has mentioned, there were other women, whose efforts and achievements, and men, whose encouragement and help, ought to have been recorded if sufficient information and space had been available; to them and their families, also, she extends her apologies.

Durham, England F. R. C. BAGLEY

A NOTE ON THE AUTHORESS

The driving force in Mrs. Badr ol-Moluk Bámdád's life has been her intense love of her country, Iran. It has inspired all her aims and pursuits and actions. It lay at the root of her passionate conviction that Iranian women must be set free.

She was born in 1905. Her father, Hájj Áqá Khán Tekini, was a keen and active supporter of the struggle for constitutional government; and it was he who first implanted ideas of freedom in her mind. These ideas were watered and nurtured by her observation of the country's then deplorable state and, in particular, the spiritual pressure, mental deprivation, and undisguised scorn of which Iranian women were then the victims. She received her primary education, and with it a knowledge of French, at home from private tutors. In 1918 she was one of the first group of students admitted to the Women's Teacher Training College.[1] From the age of fourteen onward, she wrote interesting articles for publication. Some of them were printed in the periodicals *Iránshahr*[2] and *Ferangestán* which were published abroad, others in *Gol-e Zard*[3] and other liberal-minded periodicals and newspapers then appearing in Tehran. Her writings revealed the inner intensity of her feelings. In her lectures and talks to women's associations and adult classes, her words came likewise from her heart and touched the hearts of her hearers.

In 1925 the Ministry of Education translated a domestic science syllabus for girls' schools into Persian from French but provided no textbook and had no teachers. Badr ol-Moluk Khánom then accepted the chair of domestic science at the Women's Teacher Training College. On the basis of her observations of the requirements of Iranian families, together with foreign theoretical and practical guidelines, she had written the first Persian book on domestic science but had found the task of getting it into print much harder. In the eyes of the education authorities of the time, anything written by a veiled woman was valueless and not even worth looking at. When no other hope remained, she decided to seek the help of a true friend of education, Rezá Khán Sardár-e Sepáh, who was then prime minister and war minister and was later to become Shah. Her request was immediately approved, and an order to print the book was sent to the Army Press. The sudden appearance of this first Persian book on the important subject of domestic science surprised and pleased men and women alike. It was selected as a textbook for all girls' secondary schools in the country. As a reward for this service, the contemporary director of education, Dr. Isá Sadiq, recommended that the Education Medal and a salary increase of five *tómáns*[4] per month should be awarded to the authoress. In those days, however, the wheels of officialdom turned slowly, and before the relevant orders were issued, Dr. Sadiq was transferred to another post, and both recommendations were consigned to the wastepaper basket. Although this left a scar on Badr ol-Moluk Khánom's heart, the many letters of thanks and appreciation which she received from educationists and parents enabled her to feel joy and pride in her achievement and encouraged her to do further writing. All her subsequent books are useful for women in one way or another. Among them is a book entitled *Manners and Morals in Social Life,* to which the late Názer ol-Shar'iat of Láhiján and the late Professor Badi' ol-Zamán Foruzánfar contributed prefaces. Her book on educational psychology, in which she examines the purpose and methods of girls' education, was used as a textbook in the Teacher Training College for many years. Among her other works are a book on cookery and dietetics and a book on teaching and training for democracy in Iran.

Mrs. Bámdád was a founder-member of the Ladies' Center, which came into being in 1935,[5] and one of the first group of women admitted as students into Tehran University in 1936,[6] when she entered the educational faculty (Higher Teacher Train-

A Note on the Authoress

ing College). After obtaining the license (bachelor of education degree) in 1940, she was appointed principal of the Women's Teacher Training College. At the end of the Second World War, she resigned from this post and went to America in 1946 to do research into educational problems which she had encountered in the course of her work. She earned the master of arts degree from Columbia University, New York, in 1948.

Badr ol-Moluk Khánom was the only woman to be appointed a member of the original Preparatory Commission on Radio Talks when Tehran Radio was opened in 1940, and for a long time she was adviser to the Radio Service on family guidance.

In 1956, together with a group of distinguished ladies mainly from the teaching profession, she founded the Women's League of Supporters of the Declaration of Human Rights. For many years the league has striven to acquaint Iranian women with the contents of this declaration.

From 1944 to 1945 (when it was suspended), she edited the periodical *Zan-e Emruz (Women Today),* which was esteemed for its high standard of journalism and effective advocacy of reforms.

She has traveled to European, American, Far Eastern and Middle Eastern countries in search of new insights into social and educational problems. In 1951 she opened the Bámdád Model School—a mixed school with a new curriculum. Despite many difficulties and much obstruction, this school paved the way for the adoption of modern teaching methods in private schools.

In 1967 she was invited to attend an international women's conference in Sweden at which ways to make anti-illiteracy work more effective were discussed. In her speech she described Iran's White Revolution, with particular reference to the beneficial effects expected from the establishment of the Literacy Corps, and also spoke of the problems of teaching children from different home environments. Summaries of her speech were broadcast on the radio and published in the press.

For many years Mrs. Bámdád was president of the Civil Rights Committee of the High Council of Iranian Women. In this capacity she worked with great zeal for the passage of the Family Protection Law of 1967.⁷ As she herself once said, her passion for social service came to her at birth and will only leave her at death.

Her work for the community has not prevented her from also fulfilling the roles of wife and mother. In 1926 she married Abu'l-Fazl Bámdád, a civil servant, and in the course of a happy marriage they had two daughters, Parvin (a distinguished poetess) and Nasrin (Mrs. As'ad Bakhtiári). Her husband passed away in 1963. Another event in Mrs. Bámdád's life was her performance of the pilgrimage to Mecca in 1970.

Mrs. Bámdád wrote the first volume of *Iranian Women from the Constitutional Revolution to the White Revolution* at short notice in the hope that it might be published in time for a United Nations conference on human rights which was opened at Tehran on 23 April 1968 by H.I.M. the Sháhansháh and attended also by H.I.M. the Empress Farah. She wished to give the younger generation a picture of the life which their veiled mothers and grandmothers had once lived, and of the efforts of the heroic women's leaders and the two brave and farsighted Pahlavi Shahs to obtain equal rights for Iranian women.

—Mrs. Shams ol-Moluk Javáher-e Kalám

NOTES

1. See p. 58.
2. An important literary and scholarly periodical, published in Berlin, 1922-1926, by Hoseyn Kázemzádeh Iránshahr. See E. G. Browne, *A Literary History of Persia*, fourth ed., Cambridge 1953, vol. 4, p. 488.
3. See E. G. Browne, *op. cit.*, p. 490.
4. The word *tómán* (originally a Mongol word meaning ten thousand) is used today with the meaning of ten riáls.
5. See p. 92.
6. See p. 97.
7. See p. 122

FROM DARKNESS INTO LIGHT

I

EQUALITY OF RIGHTS—
A Long-Standing Human Aspiration

Research shows that aggression and power-seeking by individuals or groups, who strive with all their might to exploit the weakness and ignorance of others, have been recurrent phenomena in human history ever since the remote past; furthermore, differences in sex, color, race, and religion have constantly been adduced as pretexts for aggression, depredation, and domination. On the other hand, philosophers and prophets who wished mankind well spared no sacrifice in their struggles to obtain mankind's acceptance of precepts which enjoin equality of individual rights; for they realized that right and justice alone can insure mankind's tranquillity and prevent wars or conflicts which destroy life and prosperity and civilization. The majority of human beings have always lacked power to defend their rights, and powerful, aggressive minorities have employed all sorts of devices to prevent their opening their eyes and casting off their blinkers of ignorance.

The great Iranian prophet Zoroaster declared that ultimately the divine power will vanquish the dark forces of Ahriman (the Devil). The revelation of the Holy Qor'án through the Prophet Mohammad not only gave men and women hope of salvation, but also taught them that human rights are ordained by God. Sooner or later the oppressed majority will react and assert their rights. Injustices and demands for their redress lay at the root of the bloodstained French Revolution, whose aims were expressed in the declaration of 1789—the Declaration of the Rights of Man. This was the first attempt to define human rights. It had no binding authority and was limited to the French nation. As soon as the fervor of the revolution died down, its principles were forgotten or ignored. Once again women were obliged to do backbreaking, underground toil in mines for a paltry reward, children were put to work at a tender age, and other injustices and abuses were perpetrated.

A second move to check inhuman aggressions and violations was the holding of an international peace conference at the Hague in 1899; but even though this resulted in the establishment of the Court of International Justice, no real advance was achieved. The same inhuman motives drove the states which had founded this court into the murderous and ruinous world war of 1914-1918. The horror caused by that war prompted the formation of the League of Nations, which after a similarly short period collapsed when the Second World War broke out in 1939. This war was the biggest worldwide disaster in history. More than ever before, the resultant anguish stirred the feelings of humane and pacific people against such evils. Calls for freedom and justice rang out from the ruins and rubble heaps. This time women endured the afflictions of war altogether equally with men and proved their worth by doing the heaviest tasks shoulder to shoulder with men for the defense of the common homeland.

Thus it is not surprising that when talk of peace began, demands for removal of every form of discrimination were eagerly and cogently raised. The most valuable result of this human upsurge was the formation of the U.N.O., and the most impressive step taken by the U.N.O. toward the achievement of lasting peace has been the issue of the Universal Declaration of Human Rights of 10 December 1948, which embodies long-held ideas of humanitarian thinkers.

In 1956, the Iranian Women's League (which had been founded in 1942) changed its name to Iranian Women's League of Supporters of the Declaration of Human Rights and specified its objective as pressure for legal enforcement of the declaration's clauses on women's rights. At the same time a program of action to this end was adopted. Every opportunity was taken to make Iranian women aware of their just deserts and to influence the younger generation in favor of complete equality and nondiscrimination, by means of lecturing, publishing of articles and slogans, and adult teaching and training.

The Universal Declaration of Human Rights includes, among its main precepts, complete equality of men's and women's rights in all social matters. The member states of the U.N.O. approved the substance of this declaration, but did not consent to be bound by it on the ground that its enforcement might cause difficulties which would have to be overcome gradually and cautiously.

Whatever may be happening in other parts of the world, Iran, fortunately, has bright prospects. With wise leadership and strong resolve, human beings can win deliverance from unjust restrictions and biases, and advance toward the lofty goals set by the Universal Declaration of Human Rights. For Iran the declaration was propitiously timed, as it came in the reign of a just and understanding Sháhansháh. H.I.M. Mohammad Rezá Sháh Pahlavi welcomed it most cordially and has shown, by his bold steps to bring about its implementation in all fields of Iranian social life, that he is truly the heir of Cyrus the Great, who proclaimed and practiced lofty ideals of humanity and justice 2,500 years ago. Indeed, the Sháhansháh pressed with more zeal than any of the world's other national leaders for its implementation not only in Iran but also elsewhere. At the same time he guided Iran into a great revolutionary transformation with such wisdom that peace and order in the country were in no way impaired.

To mark the anniversary of the Universal Declaration, and in anticipation of the conference of the United Nations Commission on Human Rights which was to be held in Tehran in May 1968 and to be opened by H.I.M. the Sháhansháh, the Iranian Women's League of Supporters of the Declaration of Human Rights decided to issue a review of the brilliant successes scored by Iranian women as a result of Iran's White Revolution of Shah and People, which since 1963 has removed all sorts of discrimination formerly imposed on women.

Now that Iranian women have won their rightful place by proving their competence in all fields of the nation's activity, besides worthily doing their vital duties as mothers and rearers of a sturdy young generation, it is time to delve into history's pages for a comparison between past and present conditions. This will contribute to the further advance of the revolution in Iranian life which began with the struggle for constitutional government (1906-1911). It will help women of today, who enjoy complete security and can see the clear highroad ahead toward a lofty social goal, to form a picture of the past, and to taste and feel some of the bitterness and blows which a handful of women in the early days of the national awakening had to endure. It will help toward an appreciation of the stubborn perseverance of the brave and noble pioneers, who stumbled up and down a dark and grueling track half a century or more ago, sometimes burning out their candle of life in the effort to reach minor goals; who felt the strong arm of organized reaction press on their bosoms to restrain them from any forward step on the path of right; who risked money and life and reputation in these struggles and, far from quitting the fray, fought on steadfastly in the hope of an opportunity to capture some bastion, however small. Mention of a number of them will be found in this book. For today's young women, who enjoy satisfactory conditions thanks to the strength and wisdom of the country's leadership in breaking old fetters and scrapping old superstitions and illusions, perhaps this book will show more clearly what a great regeneration or revolution Iran has undergone. Perhaps, in the light of what they read here, they will take pride in all these wonderful advances; and, perhaps, in gratitude for the happiness and blessings which are their lot, they will carry on the struggle to make all Iranian women aware of women's rights and duties, to reform the confused behavior patterns of backward families, to save people from the outworn forms of the past. The women of today, who do not lack insight, must still vigilantly protect Iranian society from distortions and unsuitable customs, and maintain a firm resolve to rear a new generation capable of building an even newer Iran.

II

IRANIAN WOMEN IN BYGONE DAYS

THE CENTURIES OF DARKNESS

> Only the women dwelt in darkness for centuries;
> they alone were sacrificed on the altar of hypocrisy.
> Forced to live in a cage and to die in a cage,
> these garden birds were not seen or heard in the garden.
> The women's pleas for justice remained unheard in their lifetimes;
> and the injustice was not hidden, but overt.
> From the poem *Zan dar Irán* (Women in Iran)
> Parvin E'tesámi

In spite of a brilliant past, in which Iranian women had at times risen to be reigning monarchs and leaders in statecraft and warfare, the practice of secluding the female half of the community spread to Iran as a result of political factors and worldwide tendencies, such as the Arab and Mongol invasions and increasing jealousy and fanaticism on the part of the men, who dreaded any sort of association between their wives and strangers. Since the women had to be allowed out of doors from time to time if necessary tasks were to be performed, the practice of making them conceal themselves under thick coverings was eventually also adopted. Thus they gradually became prisoners, confined in the home or under the veil and the cloak *(chádor)*. In their ignorance and isolation, they remained unaware of their own capabilities and spiritual worth. They saw themselves as feeble herbs in society's garden, only able to survive when shaded from the sunshine by robust trees, or when dependent like parasites on strong, healthy plants from which they drew sustenance. Even so, there were sometimes a few who kept alive the flame of intelligence and thereby brightened the pleasure haunts of the mighty like candles at a banquet. There were occasions when sad but beautiful verses from one of these cloistered beings seeped out through the walls of the harem and stirred the literary world to admiration; but more often such mental outpourings remained unrecorded except in her own heart and unheard except by her fellow harem inmates.

When we look back at the past and study the fate of Iran's formerly veiled and secluded women, our first impression is that they were like powerless dolls, stuck in the harem with a horizon no broader than its four walls. The poor creatures were wholly dependent on others, namely on the men who were their breadwinners and masters, and wholly ignorant of what went on outside the house. They could look forward to nothing except enslavement to the wishes of husbands or obedience to the orders of fathers and brothers. Seldom if ever did they express opinions or wishes of their own, or identify themselves with the new ideas spreading among the people of Iran, from whom they lived apart.

Sometimes, when clever and attractive women intervened secretly in the politics of their family or country, they succeeded through careful calculation in achieving their ambitions. The men, who did not credit women with any sort of ability, described such shrewdness and sagacity as "women's wiles" and warned people against them. Expecting nothing from their wives except submissive bows and absolute obedience, they not only mocked and sneered at any sign of perceptivity and rationality in a woman, but even interpreted it as in some way culpable like forgery or fraud.

This state of affairs continued until opposition against the decadent autocratic regime of the Qájár Sháhs arose and in the end prevailed. Women as well as men joined in the struggle for constitutional government and national freedom (1906-1911). The fire which had been smouldering under the ashes of centuries in Iranian women's hearts then burst into flames.

THE FIRST SIGNS OF WOMEN'S AWAKENING

Even before that time we find to our surprise that Iranian women sometimes took a firm stand. During the long reign of Náser ol-Din Sháh Qájár (1848-1896), many concessions had been granted to foreigners, and in 1891 a concession for a tobacco monopoly was granted to an English company. On this occasion the people of Iran, who had never previously questioned the commands of their rulers or dared to challenge them, with one accord gave up tobacco as soon as Hájj Mirzá Hasan Shirázi of Sámarrá in Iraq, who was then the senior clergyman of the Shi'ite Islamic religion, issued a ruling which forbade its use while the concession lasted. Náser ol-Din Sháh not only failed to quell this revolt of the country's men and women against the contract which he had signed; he also failed to subdue the women of his own harem, who smashed their *qalyán*s (waterpipes) in defiance of their royal benefactor's express command and absolute power. When the shah smoked a *qalyán* in the presence of his favorite wives and ordered them to follow his example forthwith, they replied: "Your Majesty, alcoholic drink is forbidden by Islam and we do not let it pass our lips. Right now tobacco has been forbidden by the senior clergy of the religion. It cannot be made licit for us by the monarch's command." They persisted in their abstention until the government was forced to cancel the tobacco concession in the following year and pay a large indemnity to the company. Naturally, the people were emboldened by their success in this affair.

In the reign of Mozaffar ol-Din Sháh Qájár (1896-1907), the national reawakening began to quicken, and the people presented various demands to the shah, one of which was for the establishment of a House of Justice. They wanted the shah to deprive the governors and potentates of the absolute powers which they misused so unjustly and tyrannically, and to transfer the authority to the House of Justice so that the people might have the right of self-defense against powerful oppressors. The shah's courtiers, however, regarded these proposals as injurious to their interests and were against acceptance. In protest, a number of enlightened Shi'ite *olamá* (clergymen), who had strong popular support, took sanctuary in December 1905 in the Shrine of Sháh Abdol-Azim at Shahr-e Rey (eight miles south of Tehran). The courtiers, in the hope of calming down the trouble, formed plans to get the *olamá* out of the shrine by hook or crook and to deal with them one by one. When these schemes became known, the people closed the bazaars, and the preachers in the mosques spoke in strong terms of the people's sufferings.

The only occasions when women could gather without obstruction were assemblies to hear sermons in the mosques or recitations of the martyrdom of the Emám Hoseyn,[1] and it was then that women learned about these events. One day when Mozaffar ol-Din Sháh was returning from the house of his intransigent prime minister Eyn ol-Dowleh, a crowd of women surrounded the royal coach shouting, "We want our clergy back. We want them here to register our marriages, our house-leases. O King of the Moslems, command that these leaders of the Moslems be respected! If the Russians and English then threaten you, all the millions of the Iranian nation will wage holy war at the bidding of these leaders of their faith. . ."[2] From that day onward, women—despite their cloaks and veils—contributed much to the struggle.

The purpose of mentioning these incidents is to show that even in those days Iranian women collectively demonstrated their feelings in critical situations when the interests of the community were at stake. The general opinion, however, was that women were sly and sharp-witted and concerned only to promote their own interests. Men used to speak of women's tricks and wiles and, instead of praising them or expressing appreciation, used to scold and rebuke them.

At the time when the women crowded round Mozaffar ol-Din Sháh's coach, a popular song had been composed, of which a part is quoted: "O just shah, the clergy have gone on pilgrimage, the people have gone to the [British] legation, the women have been taken into captivity. When will there be any protection against injustice? When will Eyn ol-Dowleh cease to be prime minister? How much longer is the country to be plundered?"

MARRIAGE AND THE VEIL

Iranians of the present generation must not be left in ignorance of the marriage customs prevalent in the early part of this century when their own parents or grandparents married. They ought to know how a young suitor had to choose his lifelong partner and companion without seeing or knowing her.

Full inquiries concerning the legality of the proposed marriage and the moral rectitude and financial worth of the young man and young woman had to be made before the hands of these two strangers were joined in, it was hoped, perpetual matrimony. The young man's sister and mother or other female relatives were the intermediaries who called at the young woman's home, not infrequently after learning of her existence from marriage brokers. In the course of the pompously ceremonial receptions given for these callers, the young woman, perspiring with embarrassment, was brought into the room and put on display like a piece of merchandise. Then the callers quickly eyed her from head to toe and exchanged a few words with her to make sure that she was not deaf and dumb. They usually also took off her head scarf to see that no part of her head was bald. As soon as the young man's relatives returned home from a matchmaking party, they separately and independently gave him their assessments of the young woman's quality and character.

Great difficulties used to arise when the young man's female relatives had different tastes and started disputing over their assessments. For example, one of them might describe the girl's eyes as black and attractive, whereupon another would interrupt and maintain that they were gray-green, small and dim. Often the young man would lose patience and implore them to fight their verbal battle elsewhere. If they could overcome their disagreements, then they might let him know their conclusion.

The marriage ceremonies were strange affairs, as the authoress herself saw when she attended one. The weddings of two brothers were being celebrated on the same night, and the two brides, after being taken to the house of the parents of their bridegrooms, attended a reception for the ladies which went on long after midnight. The sister of the bridegrooms, who recognized the brides (having previously seen and approved them), was busy saying good-bye to the guests; so the elderly mother of the bridegrooms hurriedly took the bit between her teeth. Thinking that the tall girl was the bride of the older boy, she led her to his room, and thinking that the short girl was the bride of the younger boy, she put her hand into his. Although the error was soon noticed and the brides were moved to the correct bridal chambers, rumor had it that the swap displeased the elder son so much that he paid no attention to his wife that night and kept his heart set on his brother's wife for the entire remainder of his life, with disastrous results for the happiness of both families.

MEN'S APARTMENTS AND WOMEN'S APARTMENTS

Another tricky matter was the way in which dwellers in the same house were supposed to deal with one another. The houses of Iranian notables were divided into two sections, the outer apartments for the master and the men servants and the inner apartments for the wives and the maids. Since women were not allowed to let their voices be heard or their hands be seen by any men except close relatives, what were the wives to do if they wished to give orders to menservants?

When eunuchs were employed in the harems, those unfortunate creatures served as intermediaries, carrying messages and news between the two parts of the house. Most women lived in constant dread of them, as a bad word or an unfavorable report from a eunuch, whether true or untrue, could reduce a wife to misery —in the Persian phrase—could "turn her bread into brick."

When the master of the house wished to enter the inner apartments, custom required that he should cough several times and say *Yá Alláh* ("O God") before crossing the threshold with downcast eyes. The ladies, when passing through the outer quarters, had to be wrapped from head to toe in *chádor*s and were expected to walk quickly and nervously.

Yet these same wives were allowed to attend recitations of the Emám Hoseyn's martyrdom,[3] sitting alongside or behind the men, and were expected to make the mourning more passionate by beating their heads and chests and uttering shrill wails. Often they brought their unweaned infants and fed them with a noxious mixture of milk, sweat and tears. Beside them were their older children, who had to sit for hours listening tearfully and with wry necks.

CONTRACTS WITH THE OUTSIDE WORLD THROUGH "BROKERESSES"

The semi-imprisoned women, who had to stay in the house from dawn to dusk and seldom went out of doors, inevitably needed contacts with the outside world. These needs were met by brokeresses. Most of them were Jewesses who wore *chádor*s but did not veil their faces, and so could walk through the streets and enter houses and speak with male members of families. They brought cosmetics, toiletries, lengths of cloth, sewing gear, gold and silver jewelry, and such to the houses for sale to the women. They also found husbands for girls. It was on the strength of their recommendations that boys sent servants to explore marriage prospects. The business was, of course, conducted with decorum, gifts and sweets being presented by both parties. The menservants or nurses were introduced to the families. Some of them used to arrange clandestine liaisons and thereby earn enormous incomes. It was amazing how often brokeresses used to carry huge sums of money or jewels in their canvas bags—sums entrusted to them in complete confidence by wealthy families for various sorts of deals. They would keep these sums overnight in their mean and insecure dwellings, and in daytime they would set out alone or accompanied by their husbands and walk unconcernedly through the streets and back alleys. The ladies in the harems would greet them cheerfully and with open arms, because their reporting of news and of other families' affairs did more than anything else to brighten the monotonous, unhealthy course of harem life. Sometimes these brokeresses became the confidantes and consolers of members of important families. They recommended, or themselves provided, magic and mumbo jumbo to relieve the sorrows and anxieties of the ladies, but, by whatever means, they cooled the fire of anguish in many a heart. It was thanks to the brokeresses that the harem women could keep themselves quite well informed about events in the city and circumstances of other families. All considered, these walking and talking newspapers were a boon to the prisoners behind the harem walls.

A FAVORITE MEETING PLACE FOR WOMEN —THE TURKISH BATH

Owners of public Turkish baths generally used to keep several women, who constituted a cost-free harem, as they earned their living, whether they were old or young. As workers they were wholly under the thumb of the bath owner, so much so that even when he was absent they did not in any way neglect their duties, as each was afraid of being reported by the others, and they were content to live on mere pittances. One woman enjoying the proprietor's trust was responsible for keeping customers' accounts and handing over the takings; she was called the mistress *(zan-e ustá)*. There were also one or more masseuses, a water carrier to bring hot water from the tank for the customers, and one or two cleaners and messengers.

The shouts and curses, complaints and squabbles of these unfortunate bath attendants, mingled with the loud chatter of the customers, the cries of their children and the banging of copper vessels such as pitchers and trays, made a most frightful din, although it seldom reached the owner's ears or disturbed him; it has made the phrase "women's bath" a common simile for tumult and hubbub. Despite this, the Turkish baths were meeting places which women gladly frequented and where they usually stayed a long time, often a whole day. They spent their time chatting together and getting and spreading news, firsthand news better than any to be found in the press. There was a proverb "use the bath water to make friends," meaning that only by pouring pitchers of water over each other's shoulders could acquaintances and friendships be gained.

"WISH-BLOUSES"[1]

On the twenty-seventh day of the lunar month of Ramazán, an extraordinary spectacle used to be seen in the Tehran mosques, especially the Sepahsálár mosque. Crowds of women gathered outside the mosque and in adjacent streets and quite seriously (for it was not meant to be funny) begged men passing by to give them money for wish-blouses. It was believed that the sewing and wearing of such blouses would bring fulfillment of women's wishes, such as to have children, to find fortunate matches for their daughters, to see their sick relatives recover and their old folk go on pilgrimage. The men treated this begging as a joke and took the opportunity to play tricks on young, veiled women. For instance, they would hold the coin which they were going to give so high up that the woman was forced to jump for it. After the begging came the sewing. The women went into the mosque in small groups and started to cut and stitch the cloth which they had bought with their takings. In the afternoon, between the noon and evening prayers, they retired behind the screen separating the two sexes in the mosque and put on their wish-blouses.

Iranian women in those days were keen buyers of magic and mumbo jumbo, talismans, prayer formulas, and the like; and impostors who exploited this ready market were numerous. Getting married and then winning her husband's trust and affection were a woman's highest hopes; for apart from her husband she had no other livelihood. It is no exaggeration to say that the Iranian woman in former times was entirely dependent on her husband; if he was kind to her, she would be happy; if he was unkind, she would be unhappy; and that was all. Consequently, she strove in all possible ways to keep her man. Being generally illiterate and ignorant, women were prone to superstition and irrationality. When a woman lost her husband, she lived a wretched life in the house of his relatives. Often, one man, whether rich or poor, fed and housed ten or fifteen female and juvenile relatives and, of course, held sway over all of them.

ABSURD RESTRICTIONS ON WOMEN

Until as late as several years after the First World War, passenger transport in Tehran was still supplied mainly by horse-drawn cabs called droshkies. There were also horse-drawn trams on a few routes. Every tram contained a women's compartment cut off by a closed door. The droshkies were subject to absurd regulations, one of which was that men and women were forbidden to ride together on the same droshky. This applied even to husbands and wives and to fathers and daughters. Whenever a woman had to be accompanied by a male relative on a visit to the doctor or any other journey, she and he were forced to ride in two different droshkies, one following the other, and as it was often difficult to find two droshkies at once, much valuable time was lost. No exceptions to this rule were allowed, even when one of the passengers was badly ill and needed the other's help.

Eventually, the leaders of the militant women's organizations brought these and other similar matters to the attention of the press, whose help they sought for a campaign against such evils; but very often their truth-telling was rewarded with libelous taunts and accusations of apostasy.

The government had furthermore imposed on every licensed droshky driver an obligation to put up the hood whenever he took on a female passenger. In 1922 a humorous newspaper named *Nesim-e Shomál* delighted its readers with a caricature showing a peasant woman mounted on a donkey and her husband, on foot with his hand on its bridle, being stopped at the approach to the city by a policeman, who turns them back saying, "Why haven't you put your donkey's hood up?"

WOMEN ONE SIDE, MEN THE OTHER

There were also regulations which stipulated that during the late afternoon and evening in busy streets of Tehran, such as

Lálezár, Sháhábád, and Amiriyeh avenues, men should walk on one side and women on the other. It was illegal for them to walk together on the same side after 4:00 P.M. If, as sometimes happened, a woman wanted to reach her own home, or some other place such as a pharmacy, which lay on the wrong side, she had to get permission from a policeman to go there. She was then allowed to cross, or to hurry out and hurry back. How often a distinguished lady had to listen to the imperious command of a policeman: "Cover your face, wench!"

HOW IRANIAN CHILDREN SHARED THEIR MOTHERS' MISERIES

In the days when Iranian mothers were imprisoned in a corner of the house and knew nothing about rights or freedom, the Iranian children and youngsters growing up beside them had to spend their formative years in idleness and mental stress. No facilities for play or exercise, no means of mind-cheering or body-strengthening amusement were provided for the children. The mothers, in their total ignorance of infant care, used to wrap the arms and legs of their innocent babies in swaddling clothes tightly bound with ribbons, and to make sure that the babies who were suffering this torture would not cry all night and deprive the parents of sleep, they used to give them doses of opium, which they called *keyf* (delight), or other addictive substances. The unfortunate children grew up in the habit of choking and weeping and groaning for hours and of making excuses and getting smacked for it. When older, the children modeled their amusements on those of the father or mother. The little girls played with dolls, i.e., they made their own dolls by sewing cotton cloths together and putting in cotton-wool stuffing and then made bridal trousseaux and household things for their dolls. All these were useful activities, but they also spent hours on end moving their dolls about and talking to them or talking for them like puppets, imitating scenes observed in the home and repeating words heard from the grown-ups. They reenacted quarrels, beatings, sulks, reconciliations, grumbles, weddings, divorces. They wept over the coming of a second wife, the loss of a husband's love, the sicknesses of other children, the misery of an empty purse. Sometimes they cooked meals in toy pots or laundered dolls' dresses.

Another pastime very popular with both girls and boys was to mimic the passion plays and martyrdom recitals.[5] Normally, they had accompanied their mothers to these gatherings and had sat cross-legged beside them for long hours, pretending to weep and lament. When left to themselves, one child would wind a piece of white cloth round his head to look like a *rowzeh-khwán*'s (rhapsodist's) turban and then start to mimic the recital, while the others would beat their chests just as adults did on these occasions. Children also pretended to act the parts of passion-play characters and tilted at each other with wooden or cardboard swords and shields which they made for themselves. Boys used to stage imitation passion plays in the streets. Other girls' pastimes were poetry competitions, recitations of stories, palmistry, and fortune-telling by means of peas. Children of aristocratic families were not permitted to enjoy the spectacles then given in open spaces and squares by jugglers, snake charmers, and professional storytellers with their colorful tableaux. More freedom was allowed to lower class children. Whenever a storyteller was performing, they could stand around and watch him.

Girls were taught from infancy onward to sit quietly, not to stir, not to ask questions, not to be curious, with the result that they became physically weakened and unattractive, and mentally incapable of self-reliance. They were trained to be humble, feeble, servile and dull. What they might do and not do was dictated to them by the male sex, even in the case of younger brothers to older sisters. Thus the dominant feelings in their minds were self-disparagement, fear and submissiveness. Most of them had seen how unhappy and abject their mothers were. Admittedly, marriages were more stable and durable in those days, when they depended on the absolute obedience and enforced patience of the wife, than they are today. If, as sometimes happened, the husband finally consented to a separation, the wife was unable to provide for her own and her children's well-being by taking a job or entering a profession. The law courts in those days showed little concern for the welfare of the children, who were left with one or the other parent and had to live in distressed and disturbed circumstances. As soon as a girl began to approach puberty, her mental peace and security were threatened. At the age of only nine she might be removed to the house of a husband and placed under the authority of a mother-in-law because her parents found the burden of her upkeep too heavy and wanted to shift it onto a husband's shoulders. The poor girl did not know what sort of a man would be given control of her fate. She was not even allowed to form an imaginary picture of him. The choice of her husband depended solely on her father's will. Suddenly, at the end of a wedding feast in which others had enjoyed the fun, she would realize that she was about to be transferred from the prison of her father's house to the custody and service of another man called her husband—"out of the frying pan into the fire."

TUTORS AND QOR'ÁN SCHOOLS

In general, the literate women of the time had learned reading and writing at home from their fathers or husbands, or from reliable, elderly private tutors who were admitted to some of the aristocratic homes. Usually in such cases much weight was given to the reading of difficult classical works, such as Rumi's *Masnavi* and Sa'di's *Golestán,* and to calligraphy, which was regarded in aristocratic families as an appropriate accomplishment for girls. Some girls also studied Arabic and composed poetry, but their number was very small. The knowledge imparted to them had a more frilly and recreational character than the subject matter taught in the old-style *maktabs* (Qor'án schools) where the schoolmaster *(mo'allem)* sat on a mattress, and his pupils—sometimes including little girls up to about age six along with boys—sat opposite him on the floor; but since those schoolmasters generally possessed little knowledge themselves and used no elementary textbooks except parts of the Holy Qor'án in Arabic, the pupils seldom acquired any competence or even a real ability to read and write. The *maktab*s served primarily as places where children could be supervised and kept out of mischief; and this task was fulfilled through the use of corporal punishment and torture, e.g., the bastinado or beating on the soles of the feet, to repress the children's ebullient spirits. Girls' schools teaching a variety of subjects in orderly conditions were not started in Iran until about the time of the struggle for constitutional government (1906-1911), and at first they were for the most part run clandestinely as classes in private homes, with teachers who were mostly men.

RELIGIOUS INSTRUCTION IN THE HAREM

In the harems of the Qájar Sháhs and contemporary grandees, the presence of a religious instructress, called *mollá-báji* or *mirzá-báji,* was generally deemed essential. Her task was to give the inmates lessons on religion and to organize or facilitate their performance of ritual duties. To the extent of her ability she also taught and trained them to write. Some of these *mollá-báji*s were learned and accomplished, especially in calligraphy. One of them, who taught in the harem of Fath Ali Shah (1796-1834), by name Mirzá Máh-Soltán Khánom, was awarded the title Amirat ol-Kottáb (Princess of the Scribes) and earned much esteem. Mirzá Máh-Sharaf Khánom, who was the sister of a religious dignitary[6] prominent in Mohammad Sháh's reign (1834-1845), wrote most of the government's decrees in her beautiful hand. Mirzá Nush-e Lab Khánom, the *mollá-báji* of Náser ol-Din Sháh's favorite wife, Anis ol-Dowleh, used to mount a pulpit in the harem and give the ladies lectures on the *Jáme'-e Abbási,* a treatise on religious law composed by Sheykh Bahá ol-Din Ámeli (1546-1622), the leading theologian and counselor of Sháh Abbás the Great. Mirzá Falak-náz Khánom, the *mollá-báji* of Shokuh ol-Soltán, who was another wife of Náser ol-Din Sháh and the mother of Mozaffar ol-Din Sháh, excelled in the *sols* style of Persian calligraphy. One of her feats was to write a sonnet by Háfez in *sols* handwriting on the inside of a rosewater bottle. She used to give calligraphy lessons by moonlight.

From old times up to the present day, there have been female *rowzeh-khwán*s (reciters of the sad events leading to the Emám Hoseyn's martyrdom). They used to be invited by the veiled ladies to recite at mourning assemblies held inside the harems and thus in former times enjoyed better patronage than now. They also used to be invited to charitable banquets given as votive offerings by families who had supplications to make. They received the utmost attention and respect on these occasions, when they gave the ladies help in phrasing prayers. The epithet *mollá*,[7] placed before the name, used to be given to these women, e.g., Mollá Maryam Khánom, Mollá Zahrá Khánom. Some of them, being particularly talented, won great fame and popularity and rose to high positions. For example, two sisters, named Mollá Gowhar and Mollá Khávar, who came from Káshán and were daughters of a master builder there named Ostád Báqer, finally joined the ranks of Náser ol-Din Sháh's consorts. Since Islam does not permit two sisters to be married simultaneously to one husband, and since there was no difference in the quality of each sister's voice and talent and beauty or in the degree of the royal affection for each, the only solution which could be found was that each in turn should be temporarily married to the shah for a period of six months. These sisters, who had lovely voices, used to sing Mowlavi Rumi's *Masnavi* to Náser ol-Din Sháh in the evenings.[8]

Another female *rowzeh-khwán* to become famous was Mollá Khadijeh Khánom, known as Máh Khánom, a daughter of Qamar ol-Molk Vaziri. Her exceptional talent brought her an outstandingly high reputation.

Today female *rowzeh-khwán*s have their professional center at the house of Mo'meneh Khánom on Shápur Avenue (intersection of Mokhtári Avenue), Tehran.

The prime minister Mirzá Hoseyn Khán Sepahsálár (who held office in 1871-1873 and unsuccessfully attempted reforms) was married to a daughter of Fath Ali Sháh, named Máh-Tábán Khánom and entitled Qamar ol-Saltaneh, who was so fond of the *rowzeh-khwán*'s art that she used to organize recitals for women in her home (later to become the house of the Iranian parliament) once a week throughout the year, in addition to the usual assemblies during the lunar months of Moharram and Safar. The reciters were always literate women with a feeling for poetry. Sometimes they performed passion plays, acting the parts of the historic-religious characters of the drama of the martyrdom in just the same way as the actors *(ta'zieh-khwáns)* in male performances. A certain Mollá Zeynab Khánom, who had a bass voice, was well known for her acting in the parts of male characters.

NOT ADDRESSING WOMEN BY THEIR REAL NAMES

After marriage a woman's greatest pride was to receive a new name, usually containing the word Áqá (today used only of men, with the meaning Mr.). Names such as Arus Áqá, Gelin Áqá, Amin Áqá, Aziz Áqá, were very popular. The giving of such a name enhanced a wife's dignity and prestige. Nevertheless, wives were not normally addressed by these names. If a wife had a son, she was usually called Naneh Hasan (Hasan's mama), Naneh Ali Áqá, and the like.

After this brief sketch of things as they were in the old days, let us pass on to look at the courage and tenacity of a number of women who woke up and then set out as pioneers to hoist a light of salvation in the path of Iranian society.

NOTES

1. Grandson of the Prophet Mohammad, second son of the Emám Ali, husband of the Iranian princess Shahrbánu (daughter of Yazdgerd III). Encouraged by a message from the people of Kufa in Iraq, the Emám Hoseyn set out from Madina with a small party and crossed the desert. They were surrounded by troops of the Caliph Yazid at Karbalá near Kufa in A.D. 680, and the Emám and many of his relatives and followers were killed. The anniversary of the martyrdom on the tenth day of the lunar month of Moharram is the most important event in the Shi'ite Moslem religious year. It is commemorated by recitations of the story *(rowzeh-khwáni)*, by mourning processions, and (now only in small towns and villages) by "passion plays" *(ta'zieh* or *shabih)*. The mourning processions are first recorded from Baghdad under the Buyids (an Iranian dynasty from the district of Deylam near Qazvin, who ruled western Iran and Iraq A.D. 945-1055). The passion plays came into vogue about the beginning of the nineteenth century. Under the Qájár Sháhs, magnificent performances were staged at a place in Tehran called the

Takiye-ye Dowlat. One bizarre feature was that since women were not allowed to show themselves to strange men, female roles had to be performed by male actors, who wore women's clothes with black cloths over their faces, thus concealing their moustaches and beards, and only had their eyes showing. They sang or recited their lines from pieces of paper, which they held in their hands while making the gestures and movements required by their parts. At the same time appropriate music was played. The men in warriors' roles wore armour and helmets and carried swords. Some actors became famous personages of their time. Passion plays were usually performed on a high platform in the middle of a large enclosure, on one side of which the veiled female spectators sat on the ground on carpets, and on the other side of which sat the male spectators, some on chairs in boxes and others on the ground.

2. From Seyyed Ahmad Kasravi's (*Tárikh-e Mashrute-ye Irán*) *History of the Constitution*, third ed., Tehran, 1344/1965.
3. See note 1.
4. *Piráhan-e morád.*
5. See note 1.
6. Hájji Mollá Mohammad Taqi Borgháni, a strictly orthodox theologian who was assassinated by a Bábi in 1847 and is designated the "Third Martyr." His (and Máh Sharaf Khánom's) niece was the celebrated poetess Qorrat ol-Eyn Táhereh, who was put to death in the repression of the Bábi movement in 1852.
7. Ordinarily given to lesser members of the Shi'ite Moslem clergy.
8. Quoted from the book *Zendegi-ye Khosusi-ye Náser ol-Din Shah* (*The Private Life of Náser ol-Din Sháh*), by Dust Ali Khán, who was a son-in-law of Náser ol-Din Sháh.

III

THE CONSTITUTIONAL REVOLUTION (1906-1911) AND WOMEN'S AWAKENING

WOMEN'S EFFORTS AND SETBACKS

Although the Constitutional Revolution was the work of the educated and enlightened class of contemporary Iranian society, it received support from the people as a whole, who had been driven to desperation by the injustice and the political and social decay experienced under the previous autocratic regime. The blinkers of ignorance were lifted from the eyes of uneducated people when they heard fiery speeches by the liberal-minded Moslem *olamá* and preachers who played a leading part in the revolution. They woke from the sleep of unconcern, in which they had so long unprotestingly borne their hard lot, and began to take notice, particularly when enlightened speakers translated and explained the precepts of the Islamic religion to the masses and insisted on disclosing to them truths which had formerly been concealed or misrepresented. The women, and even the men, came to realize that just as Islam does not exclude or exempt women from any of its religious or ritual obligations, so likewise does it not deprive women of any of the human rights and, furthermore, that the founder of the religion not only emphasized that women have personality and dignity, but also showed special concern for the position of mothers and emphasized the need to equip them with high standards of knowledge and awareness. Iranian women began to open their eyes and look beyond the narrow confines of their environment, beyond the walls of the harem and the thick opacity of the veil, to a broader horizon. They smelled the perfume of liberty and heard the congenial themes of right and law.

The emancipationist caravan was headed by leaders who for many years had maintained contact with the European countries and seen their steadily increasing progress, and who, consequently, perceived the terrible harm caused by the debarment of Iranian women from civilization's advance. At that critical time it was essential that the women's considerable strength should be mobilized for participation in the general struggle; and in the longer view it was essential that the women should rear the next generation to desire freedom and live in freedom and to reject any revival of autocracy and tyranny and injustice, which would shake the foundations of their homes. There was a special need to help superstitious families who were incapable of accepting guidance from the traveled and enlightened younger people.

In the event, the country's qualified women gave ample proof of their innate strength and fulfilled their duties beyond the limits of expectation. In those perilous days when the constitutionalists were battling to cast out the ogre of autocracy, these women contributed all they could to the struggle. To everyone's great surprise, it was observed that wherever men gathered in desperation to demand justice and equality and respect for rights, invariably also present would be some women—some of those creatures hitherto regarded as inert dolls and mere playthings for men who called them "weak ones," and as so unintelligent that any sign of initiative or ingenuity in them evoked ridicule. They came with veils over their faces and cloaks over their bodies, but they then twisted their white veils round their necks and pulled out weapons from under their black *chádor*s and faced the bullets and the bayonets while urging and helping their sons and husbands to stand firm.

This is attested by the following passages from H.I.M. the Sháhansháh's book *The White Revolution* (Tehran, 1967) and W. Morgan Shuster's book *The Strangling of Persia* (New York, 1912).

The Constitutional Revolution and Women's Awakening

Reference must be made [H.I.M. the Sháhansháh writes], and the highest tribute of respect must be paid, to the innate personality and strength of character of the women of Iran, who even in our community's darkest phases proved their worth in various fields and radiated the spiritual light peculiar to the Iranian genius in various ways. One conspicuous example of this in the modern political and social history of Iran can be seen in the events of 1911. Not long before then, the Russian and British governments had divided Iran into spheres of influence by their notorious treaty of 1907. When the Iranian government attempted to reform the country's fiscal and tax system by engaging an American expert, Morgan Shuster, and when he showed by his actions that he was a conscientious and disinterested official, the Tsarist Russian government, being averse to any improvement in Iran's unhealthy financial condition, presented the Iranian government with a 48-hour ultimatum demanding his expulsion and simultaneously sent troops into northern Iran. This ultimatum gave rise to various national demonstrations in the country, of which the most impressive was a public demonstration by a large number of Iranian ladies.

Shuster himself writes in his interesting book:

Special commendation must be given to the veiled women of Iran—women kept in seclusion by an impenetrable wall of social customs, deprived of any social or intellectual independence, allowed no opportunity to acquire knowledge or mental training, but filled nevertheless with an intense love of their country. When rumours spread that Iran's parliamentary deputies had decided in secret session to surrender to the threat of force, it was this love of their country which made the women respond to the foreign insult with manly courage. At the same hour of the same day, three hundred of them walked out of their homes and their barred harems, with glowering expressions and in many cases with pistols hidden under their black *chádor*s, and made their way to the Majles (parliament), where they tore off their veils and declared that rather than see the deputies timidly and cravenly let the nation's dignity be trampled underfoot, they would kill the deputies and their own husbands and children and themselves so that at least the corpses might vouch for Iran's honour.

H.I.M. the Sháhansháh adds, "How could such women still be deemed unfit to share in the life of the community?"

Many other instances of the selfless devotion of Iran's veiled women are recorded in history's pages, and some will be cited in this book.

During the term of the first Majles (1906-1908), the government submitted a proposal for the acceptance of a loan of fifteen million *qerán*s (riáls) from a foreign power to meet current expenditure. The deputies took the view that Iran was already too deep in debt and refused to authorize further borrowing. When the government persisted, on the ground that it would otherwise be unable to pay its regular outgoings and the salaries of its officials, some of the deputies suggested the raising of an internal loan and the establishment of a national bank as better ways to solve the problem. On hearing this news, women offered their earrings, bracelets and necklaces to raise the capital for the national bank. One woman came into the grounds of the Majles and said, "I work as a laundress, and I have only one *tomán* of savings. Accept this *tomán* for what it is worth and for what it means, so that I too may subscribe to the national bank." This moving incident is mentioned in Seyyed Ahmad Kasravi's detailed history of the struggle for constitutional government.

Women also had secret societies at that time. In *The Strangling of Persia,* Shuster makes the following observation: "When women in Europe and America form societies, nobody feels any surprise; but veiled Moslem women in Iran carry on secret political activities in their societies." As an example, he mentions:

> Once my wife and I were invited to a reception for foreigners. An Iranian member of my staff advised me not to go to the party because a conspiracy was afoot, and I did not go. On making inquiries, I found out that he had been right, and afterwards I asked him how he had learnt about the affair. He replied that his mother belonged to a secret society of Iranian women, in which all sorts of moves were being made to thwart the intrigues of traitors to the country; and one of the society's actions was to gather information about me because I was a pro-Iranian foreign adviser.

It was in recognition of such instances of patriotic devotion in that time of tense excitement and fanaticism and plotting that the nation's leaders, when drafting the constitution,[1] adopted the principle of universal suffrage and eligibility for election. They did not disqualify women in any way, or mention any disabilities of women in the legal and political fields. Afterward, however, in the election law of July 1909, the eligibility rules specifically denied the suffrage to women, along with minors and other persons (such as lunatics) under tutelage, and criminal bankrupts and offenders, convicted robbers and murderers, and offenders sentenced to Islamic legal penalties. Thus the denial of human rights to women was officially maintained, and its harmful effects continued to be seen in the legislation which was passed and the way the young generation was brought up.

Nevertheless, the preaching of the liberal-minded leaders and the self-sacrifice of the women during the struggle for constitutional government had lasting consequences. Large numbers of sensible Iranians were awakened, and among them were a number of courageous and clear-headed women who kept the yearning for freedom foremost in their hearts. Although their path was inevitably long and full of pitfalls, they persevered steadfastly. Through their efforts the foundations of the Iranian women's renaissance were firmly laid. The schools and the societies which they founded, the articles which they wrote, and the journals which they published significantly influenced the later course of events; but since the Iranian government was unable in those days to give them any effective support, and since the building of a new social structure would in the then-existing conditions have been impossible without extraordinarily strong rule and guidance, it looked at first as if the efforts of these women would be frustrated by their antagonists and produce no concrete results.

THE WOMEN'S FREEDOM SOCIETY

By the time of the grant of the constitution (on 30 December 1906), a considerable number of Iranians had, as already mentioned, gained knowledge of modern civilization through travel abroad and contact with Europeans. Some of them then began to think about ways of accustoming the country's women to attend gatherings in which men took part and thereby getting women interested and involved in matters of concern to the whole community. After long and earnest discussions and exchanges of ideas, they reached the decision to establish the Women's Freedom Society[2] and drew up rules for it. These permitted men accompanied by their wives or daughters or other relatives to attend the society's meetings, but strictly forbade the attendance of single men or women.

The society's meetings were to be held twice a month in places outside Tehran's city boundaries where the coming and going of the members would attract less attention. Its discussions were to be centered solely on the status and problems of the country's women. The task of lecturing or speaking at the meetings would be reserved to the women members, so that the women themselves might choose subjects for discussion and propose solutions for their problems. The purpose of the society's organizers was to accustom women to the appropriate deportment at mixed gatherings and discussions on important matters, especially the vital problems of family life, and at the same time to help women to overcome shyness and embarrassment.

The most prominent ladies in this society, according to one of its members who quoted their names from memory, were: Mirzá Báji Khánom, the wife of Naváb Sami'i, Sadiqeh Dowlatábádi, Monireh Khánom, Gelin Khánom Mováfeq, Eftekhár ol-Saltaneh and Táj ol-Saltaneh (two daughters of Náser ol-Din Sháh), Afsar ol-Saltaneh, Mr. Hakim's wife, Shams ol-Moluk Javáher-e Kalám, Dr. Ayyub's wife, Efendiyeh Khánom, Mrs. Jordan, Fakhr ol-Moluk daughter of Shaykh ol-Rayis Qájár. There were also a few others.

Since Fisherábád (now a section of Tehran near the U.S. Embassy) then lay outside the city boundaries, the ladies reckoned that a garden and florist's shop named Protiva on Fisherábád Avenue would be a suitable venue for their meetings. The association's executive committee negotiated with the proprietor and obtained his permission. One day when a meeting was being held, after sunset and with the strict secrecy always maintained in the society's activities against the risk of being denounced as

The Constitutional Revolution and Women's Awakening

infidels and molested by ruffians, a man appeared and asked permisson to join the society alone, without his wife. His request was not accepted, as it was contrary to the society's rules. The man took offense and hurried away and informed some fanatical *mollá*s living at the lower end of the Tehran bazaars. Soon a large crowd was on the march from the Abbásábád bazaar, where one of these *mollá*s lived, up toward Fisherábád. Naturally, the police did nothing to stop them. God helped the women, however. Before the crowd reached the city gate, an Armenian youth named Ághási, who was an apprentice in the then-well-known photography studio of Antoine Khán, noticed what was going on and bicycled with all possible speed to the Protiva garden just in time to avert a very nasty incident.

The mood of the society's members, and especially its women members, can be imagined. They fled and hid in various places. The scoundrels and ruffians who had come to insult and attack them went home disappointed after finding the garden empty.

This was one of the ordeals undergone by the group of modern-thinking workers for change in women's status. Nothing came of their efforts and plans, however, and they had to give up and admit defeat. This was due to their own fewness and to the lack of sympathy for their lofty objectives in prewar ruling circles.

A CONSTITUTIONALIST PRINCESS IN A SECRET SOCIETY

Not without surprise we learn that one of the leading women campaigners in the struggle for constitutional government was a daughter of Náser ol-Din Sháh named Maleke-ye Irán, who was the wife of Zahir ol-Dowleh. She belonged to a *darvish* order, and their daughters Forugh ol-Moluk and Malak ol-Moluk wore the *darvish* costume and headgear and carried the begging bowl and the mace. They let themselves be photographed in this with their faces uncovered. On the anniversary of the birth of Safi Ali Sháh (head of the Ne'matolláhi *darvish* order, d. 1924), Zahir ol-Dowleh, whose birthday fell on the same date, gave a commemoration party in the monastery of the *darvish*es, and the gathering attracted many men and women from among the order's following. Maleke-ye Irán was present, together with her daughters, and she recited a poem, of which the following verses are a part:

> The birthday of Safi is the birthday of sincerity (*safá*).
> Both bring happiness to the poor, to the *darvishes*.
> I love this festival which sincerity has launched.

Maleke-ye Irán was a woman with strong sentiments, and she composed a song about the ruined state of the country in those days which became very popular and was sung by men and women of all classes. Some lines from the song, which did a lot to sharpen the people's patriotic feelings, follow:

> We sleepers now are waking up, may be?
> You say, dear friend, "It never can be so!"
> We'll be efficient, like the Americans?
> You say, dear friend, "It never can be so!"
> And like Japan, renowned for every skill?
> You say, dear friend, "It never can be so!"

The fact that Maleke-ye Irán was an ardent constitutionalist and patriot did not escape the notice of the despotic Mohammad Ali Mirzá, who succeeded to the throne in January 1907 and was deposed in July 1909. One of his actions after he had bombarded the Majles (parliament) building and suspended the constitution in June 1908 was to order the wrecking and pillage of Maleke-ye Irán's house. It should be mentioned that Zahir ol-Dowleh was head of a constitutionalist secret society, the Okhuvat (Brotherhood) Society, and that Maleke-ye Irán used to go to its meetings unveiled and speak at them.

NÁSER OL-DIN SHÁH'S LIBERAL-MINDED, FAVORITE DAUGHTER

Náser ol-Din Sháh's favorite daughter, Táj ol-Saltaneh, was an educated, well-informed and very sensitive woman. She was unhappy in her married life, which soon ended in divorce. She then had to face many difficulties and anxieties. Her daughters were taken away from her to live with their father's next wife. Perhaps the conflicts and misfortunes of her life were what gave her breadth of outlook and depth of feeling about her earlier and later circumstances. In the memoirs which she has left, she deplores the unsystematic and unsuitable nature of her own and her husband's educations and the guile of the flatterers who surrounded her. She also deplores the unhappy state of the people in the reigns of her father and her brother (Mozaffar ol-Din Sháh), and the shocking class differences which then existed. She attributes her father's murder (in 1896) to the injustices and intrigues and crimes of the courtiers on whom he relied. She expresses belief in freedom and equality of rights for all citizens of the nation, and loathing of the oppressive and unjust ways in which the strong then treated the weak.

As already mentioned, Táj ol-Saltaneh played an active part in one of the reformist movements, namely the Women's Freedom Society.

This beautiful woman spent the last years of her life on the bed of sickness, suffering intense and almost unbearable pain, but thanking God and trusting that this penance for her sins in the lower world would save her in the world above.

THE FIRST PUBLIC DEMONSTRATION BY WOMEN

On one of the critical days through which Iran passed in November and December 1911, after the Russians had sent an ultimatum demanding the dismissal of the government's American financial adviser, Morgan Shuster, hundreds of women demonstrated outside the parliament building. Clad in lugubrious black *chádor*s and white veils—though one of them, who was a royal (Qájár) lady, had a national flag draped over her shoulders—they presented a sad yet stirring spectacle. After hearing a patriotic poem, composed and recited by Mrs. Zeynab Amin, they cried out with one voice: "Independence or Death!"

How had it become possible for Iranian women to acquire such ardent feelings and express them in such a forceful way?

In 1910 the wife of a veteran constitutionalist and patriot, Seyyed Kázem Rashti, had invited a number of enlightened ladies to her house to discuss the disastrous condition of the country and the deplorable status of its women. One of those who came was the wife of Yeprem Khán (the Armenian Iranian leader of the volunteer force which had helped to restore constitutional government in July 1909 and who later became chief of police), who had just returned to Tehran from Tabriz. Altogether about sixty persons were present, and their national feelings were deeply stirred; so much so that at the end of the gathering they joined hands to show their unity and swore to devote their minds solely to the troubles of their beloved country. They arranged to continue meeting once a week for the purpose of deciding on further plans, and they were invited to hold their next gathering at the house of Mrs. Zeynab Amin's father, Áqá Seyyed Abdolláh "Atábeki," who was a poet and a keen constitutionalist. It was there that after several speeches and a long debate the foundations of an organized body called the National Ladies Society[3] were laid.

At its first meeting, the following persons were chosen to form the executive committee: Mrs. Ághá Beygom, daughter of Áqá Sheykh Hádi Najmábadi, president; Mrs. Ághá Sháhzádeh Amin, treasurer; and Miss Sadiqeh Dowlatábádi, secretary.

The membership, which included some well-known personalities, was as follows: the wife of Mirzá Soleymán Khán Meykadeh; the mother of Dr. Mahdi Khán Meykadeh; the wife of Malek ol-Motakallemin (mother of senator Dr. Malekzádeh); Mrs. Nozhat Jahángir; Effat ol-Moluk Khwájeh Nuri; Nazm ol-Moluk Khwájeh Nuri; the wife of Seyyed Kázem Rashti; Zeynab ol-Dowleh; Golshan ol-Moluk Qahramáni, and Irán Khánom wife of E'telá ol-Molk, daughters of Moshár ol-Saltaneh Qadimi; the wife of Mirzá Kázem Khóshnevis; the wife of Sadiq ol-Saltaneh; a daughter of Sardár Afkham; a daughter of Sepahsálár Tonákábuni; the wife of Mofakhkham ol-Mamálek; the wife of Hájj Mirzá Hasan; a sister of Sheykh ol-Molk Owrang (she had been awarded the title Nattáq ol-Nesván); Dorrat ol-Ma'áli (founder of the Dorrat ol-Madáres School); Homá Mahmudi; Máh-Rokh Gowharshenás, sister of Modir-e Sanáye'. A number of others subsequently joined from time to time.

These zealous and ardent ladies made frequent speeches about the independence of the motherland and the need to strengthen the constitutional regime and cooperate with the constitutionalist movement. Since they attributed Iran's contemporary misfortunes to foreign influences, they were opposed to the importation of foreign goods and acceptance of loans from foreigners, and to any sort of action which might promote foreign interference in the country's internal affairs.

The first steps which they took were to wear dresses of Iran-made cloth and to establish an orphange on Bágh-e Vahshi Avenue (now Ekbatán Avenue). To raise the necessary funds, they held a great garden party, exclusively for women, at the house of Aziz Khán Khwájeh (Nosrat ol-Soltán). This brought in a large sum, and most of the prominent men of the time also gave substantial help. Sepahdár Tonákábuni[4] presented a wooded plot on what is now Valiábád Avenue to the society, and with the proceeds of the garden party they built a school for orphans on this site. One hundred orphaned girls were accommodated and educated in the school, free of charge. An Armenian Iranian lady, the wife of Mátávus Khán Malekiáns, was chosen to be headmistress, and in order that Moslem girls might be admitted, she likewise went to work in a *chádor* and with a veil covering her face. Eventually the school was handed over to the Ministry of Education.

Later in the same year, on 29 November 1911, the Imperial Russian government sent its ultimatum, and the Iranian government finally had to submit and dissolve the Majles on 24 December 1911. The crisis prompted the National Ladies' Society to organize a large public meeting on 1 December 1911 outside the Baharestán palace, where the Majles was in session. Thousands of cloaked and veiled women appeared on the scene, and successive spokeswomen mounted the rostrum and made fervent speeches in defense of the constitutional regime and in favor of national independence and social justice.

Mrs. Zeynab Amin, who was a teacher at the Shábábád Girls' School, was led to the rostrum by a well-known preacher, Áqá

Bahá ol-Váʻezin. She recited the following poem which she had composed:

> O unworthy sons of our fathers,
> death is better than life without honor!
> Life depends on good repute,
> and is indecent without it!
> Woe to you who feel no anguish,
> who lack courage and manhood!
> A body without veins is mere dust,
> nay, dust is better than such a body!
> If a man has pride and self-respect,
> how can he feel such fear of Russia?
> Now is the time for sacrifice, for manly courage,
> not for inert, weak-minded timidity!
> Let us fight like lions, like heroes
> Let us adorn this age with good repute!
> Now is the time for action! Be brave!
> Islam will advance. Let us advance with it!

The poems, speeches and slogans uttered by these veiled ladies roused the crowd to such a pitch of enthusiasm and excitement that they all cried out: "Independence or death!"

On the following day, the group of ladies went to the telegraph office and sent telegrams to the governments of all countries complaining of the Imperial Russian government's action. Thence they walked to the house of the eminent constitutionalist statesman Hájj Ali Qoli Khán Sardár Asʼad Bakhtiári, where one of them, the wife of Eʼtemád ol-Hokamá, made the following speech:

> Fellow citizens! Insofar as we Iranians have a duty to act in a courteous and conciliatory way with this unscrupulous and greedy neighbor, we have indeed so acted. Up to the limits of possible endurance, we have borne with this neighbor's vicious, brutal, murderous and arrogantly oppressive conduct. With the compliance of our own self-indulgent rulers and venal ministers, the Russians have taken away our independence and dignity. They have not reckoned that this long-ailing country will revive and regain sufficient strength to breathe freely. Every hour they cast rocks in the path of our recovery, every minute they put up bar-

riers against our progress. Not content with this, they have now presented an ultimatum filled with Iran-destroying demands and accompanied by threats. In such a situation, every person who has feelings of conscience, patriotism and self-respect will necessarily refuse to submit to the humiliation, to endure the shame and disgrace. As long as he or she lives, it is his or her duty to defend the country, to protect its honor against violation by foreigners. In other words, he or she must be prepared to fight and die, and in so doing to leave a great and worthy name in the record of history.

Dear Ladies! Have no fear! Strive to keep our country's pure soil untrampled by alien boots!

The speech ended amid rapturous applause from the ladies. During the next few days most of them eagerly arranged to sell their jewelry and gold ornaments and implements, for the purpose of helping the government pay off its debt to Tsarist Russia and thereby freeing the country from the heavy loan burden, which they thought was the main source of Tsarist Russian influence in Iran.

The patriotic spirit and the feeling of revulsion against foreign interference stirred the ladies so deeply that in the following days they succeeded in persuading the tea shops to close, so that consumption of imported foreign sugar might be cut, and in compelling passengers on the horse-drawn trams (which were the most comfortable means of street transport in those days) to get off because the tram company was foreign-managed; they then urged the passengers to go by cab instead and even paid their cab fares.

On Wednesday, 5 December 1911, the National Ladies' Society sent the following telegram to the Majles:

From the National Ladies' Society to the exalted National Consultative Assembly, may God strengthen its foundations!

The duty of parliamentary deputies is to determine the nation's laws, to keep watch on the policies of the ministers, and to supervise the activities of the government's agents. In nearly a year and a half of valuable time, what has been done? Russian troops are now permanently stationed in our territory. The English without justification send unfriendly and inhumane notes and threaten us.

Our system of justice is so chaotic that Buddhists or even uncivilized barbarians—if shown our laws—would be too horrified to look at them, let alone to accept them. When a nation has had no permanent code for 1300 years, what difference does capricious, ephemeral legislation make?

Why is it that necessary steps for expulsion of the Russian troops have not been and are not being taken?

Why is nothing being done to make our roads and cities safe, and thereby to deprive the enemy of pretexts for intervention?

Why do not you clear up the administration of justice, and stop the expenditure of millions on bonuses and remissions?

Why is no planning for the future undertaken, when particular steps are bound to run up against general impediments?

Now that the harvest is finished, why do not you start immediate investigations to find out who are the persons who are ruthlessly forcing our poor nation to eat such expensive and inferior bread?

The nation is exhausted and at its last breath. If you cannot truly shoulder your burden of service to the country, you should withdraw. When the nation is so concerned over its disastrous position, either you must undertake to establish order and prosperity within a specified time, or, if you cannot do so within that time, you must resign so that the nation may be saved by other hands.

At this juncture, the Russian Legation issued the following circular:

To the respected Ladies of Iran, long may they thrive!

Since the present status of women in Iran is such that they cannot freely express political opinions on behalf of the general public, the ladies are respectfully requested to go to the trouble of answering the following questions:

1. Has the principle of constitutional government in Iran in any way changed the status of Iranian women? If it has caused a change, what is the nature of the change? If it has not caused a change, what is the reason?

2. Do the women of Iran prefer constitutional government to the previous system? If so, why do they prefer it, and if not, why not?

3. Are Iranian women content with their present status and position, and if not, why not?

The Constitutional Revolution and Women's Awakening

4. Do they consider the status of European women preferable to their own position, and if so, why?

5. By what means and in what form do they hope to see their worth and dignity improved?

Ladies who desire that their names shall not be disclosed are requested to indicate this, instead of signing at the bottom of the form.

The answers to the Russian questionnaire given by the National Ladies' Society were as follows:

1. Being strong or weak obviously produces effects. Insofar as the constitutional regime in Iran has lacked strength, it has to that extent failed to open many girls' schools or offer much scope to women who prefer civilization and education to lack of skills and idleness.

2. Every person who has a sound conscience prefers justice and legality to autocracy and arbitrary misrule. This attitude is shared by men and women alike.

3. We are not content with our status and position. We are the victims of unruliness and lack of law.

4. We consider the position of European women preferable because they possess skills, but not for any other reasons.

5. We hope that our position will be improved through the enactment of a code of equality, because human worth and dignity are secured by the spread of law and in no other way.

It must be admitted that in the demonstrations which have just been described women's rights were not the only issue. United in heart and voice, the women made known their desire that the country should be saved from arbitrary tyranny and that the public's sufferings should be relieved; but at the same time they gave notice of their own existence and showed how important their cooperation could be.[5]

A certain royal (Qájár) lady, speaking of these demonstrations in which she herself took part, said to the authoress:

The pioneers of women's militancy in that past age made tremendous sacrifices. They exposed their breasts to arrows of accusation and reproach flung by women and men of the common people, who denounced them as "wantons," "Bábis" and "apostates." They never took offense or lost heart. They knew that for centuries imperialists seeking influence and power in this country had held back the flow of knowledge and culture, so that a dark mist of ignorance and illiteracy and corrupting propaganda might prevent Iranians from seeing the light of truth. That is why these ladies considered it their duty to open schools. Education would make Iranian women aware of their legitimate rights and give them additional strength for a more vigorous national struggle. At the same time these ladies kept in mind their own special goal, which was to win freedom and happiness for women. Moreover, in those days the teaching profession was the only field in which an Iranian woman could attain a position of importance and win renown.

THE UNKNOWN WOMAN SOLDIER

In January 1963 an article appeared in the magazine *Taraqqi* under the heading "Secrets of the Iranian Struggle for Constitutional Government." From it is taken the following account of the killing of a woman patriot by ruffians in the Meydán-e Tupkháneh (now Meydán-e Sepáh):

In November 1907 a crowd of gangsters and tough guys and state-employed muleteers and camel drivers, all in the pay of Mohammad Ali Sháh who was in conflict with the constitutional regime, gathered in the Meydán-e Tupkháneh, shouting "Down with the constitution!" They were joined by a handful of purported *mollá*s, also hirelings of the royal court. At that time tents and cauldrons used to be set up in the Meydán-e Tupkháneh for the issue of free suppers and lunches to partisans of autocracy, while nationalists used to gather at the gate of the parliament house and in the adjacent Sepahsálár mosque, where they made ready to defend themselves. Every day in the Meydán-e Tupkháneh some prominent partisan of autocracy would make a speech urging people to destroy the Majles and overthrow the constitution. One day a young man named Mirzá Enáyatolláh, who held a secure and well-remunerated position and was wearing a gold watch with a gold chain, walked into the Meydán-e Tupkháneh, and the ruffians, as soon as they caught sight of his gold watch and chain, swarmed around him yelling, "He's a constitutionalist." With this excuse they went for him and finished him off, at the same time plundering his watch and the money in his pocket and everything he had on him, including his clothes. Not content with that, one of the murderers then walked up to the bloodstained corpse and cut out the eyes with a penknife and shouted, "Bear witness that it was I who cut out the constitutionalist's eyes from his skull after his death!" This dreadful sight made all the spectators tremble; but the only one who uttered a sound was a woman, who drew a pistol from under her cloak and fired it at the murderers. She used up all the bullets without hitting anybody. This brave deed infuriated the murderers. All at once they pounced on her and tore her to pieces with daggers and swords and did atrocious things to her, which being contrary to Islamic precepts shocked the *mollā*s present at the scene.

After quoting this report (from a book having the same title), the magazine commented that there would indeed be good reason to record the name of this devoted lady as the unknown woman soldier who gave her life in the nation's war for freedom; but unfortunately the identity of this Iranian Joan of Arc, whose abominable murder took place in broad daylight before the eyes of thousands of people, is not known. Perhaps her relatives were so smitten by the same horror which smote all those present that they did not dare to reveal their kinship or mention her name.

THE FIRST GIRLS' SCHOOLS

It was during the years of struggle for constitutional government that the first schools in Tehran offering a broad, modern education to Moslem girls were opened. These schools were private. Although the principle of compulsory education at state expense was enshrined in the constitution (article nineteen of the Supplementary Fundamental Law of 1907) and in an education law passed by the second Majles in 1910, state schools for girls only came into being after the First World War. The changing cabinets which took over the government were short of money and absorbed in successive crises, while the small but growing minority of Iranians who saw the need for girls' education were inclined to inertia. The great majority of the people clung to traditional attitudes.

Some of these schools began as tutorial classes in private homes, others were founded and run by patriotic ladies who defied the environment. When official recognition was obtained—often not without difficulty—from the Ministry of Education, the schools came under the ministry's supervision (as required by the same article of the constitution).

It is noteworthy that these pioneer headmistresses were not only Iranian patriots but also devout and practicing Moslem believers. Valuable pioneering work was also done by the American Girls' School and the Ecole Franco-Persane. Their achievements are briefly described in the following paragraphs.

A RESOLUTE PIONEER

One of the outstanding pioneers of girls' education was Mrs. Tubá Ázmudeh, who founded the Námus School in 1907, not long after the grant of the constitution and at a time when conditions in the country were very disturbed. Since her action conflicted with the interests and feelings of the reactionaries, there was a constant risk that this new educational institution might be swept out of existence by a wave of calumnies and cries of apostasy, which carried weight in those days. In fact, the devoted founder had to face threats to her life and aspersions on her respectability and honor. Defamatory songs in versified slang accusing the girls of unchastity were composed and spread around. Nevertheless, this resolute lady showed such sangfroid and tenacity that she succeeded not only in keeping the Námus School in existence but also in making it one of the biggest and best-equipped schools in the country, with spacious premises on what is now Shápur Avenue. Offering the complete range of secondary curricula, this school became an important nucleus of girls' education. Tubá Khánom also started classes at the school for adult women. Her well-grounded conviction that women's education, far from being contrary to Islam, is rooted in its principles, was

The Constitutional Revolution and Women's Awakening

demonstrated by the teaching of Qor'ánic and other religious texts in all classes and the holding of commemorative recitations during the annual days of mourning for the Emám Hoseyn's martyrdom.

An aspect of the matter which should not be overlooked is the difficulty of getting teachers for girls' schools in those days. Women with good education and aptitude to teach were simply not available, while employment of male teachers would have provoked a hue and cry likely to end in closure of the school. Tubá Khánom was not deterred. Through her husband, she invited elderly male scholars to her home to coach girls for the very severe examinations which sixth-year primary-school pupils had to take in those days. The first group of pupils who successfully completed their courses at the Námus School consisted of Turán Ázmudeh (Tubá Khánom's niece, later Mrs. Ámuzgár), Fakhr-e Ozmá Arghun, Bibi Khánom Khalvati, Gilán Khánom, Farkhondeh Khánom, and Mehrangiz Sami'i. They are all accomplished persons and were among the girls who succeeded in obtaining the official certificate of education (for secondary-school teaching).

There is a story worth telling about the way in which Tubá Khánom obtained her own education. She was born in 1878, and when she reached the age of fourteen her father, Mirzá Hasan Khán Sartip, arranged her marriage to a fellow army officer, Abdol-Hoseyn Mir Panj, who had scholarly inclinations. The couple had no children, and the difference in age between them was very large. In order to keep his wife occupied, the husband encouraged her to study Persian, Arabic and French with private tutors. No sooner had she become aware of the value of knowledge than she resolved to implant and nurture it in the minds of the girls of her time. She devoted her entire energy to serving the community in this way, and her success in fulfilling the onerous task which she had set herself assures her name an honored place in the pages of history. She died in 1936, after a lifetime in which a considerable number of girls had successfully completed their primary and secondary studies under her supervision and had then for the most part continued to serve the cause of education by teaching in girls' schools. Among the men who supported

Tubá Khánom in this cause, Seyyed Javád Sartip, Mirzá Hoseyn Roshdiyeh,[6] Nasir ol-Dowleh, and Adib ol-Dowleh particularly deserve mention. Tubá Khánom's great-nephew, Dr. Jamshid Ámuzgár, was finance minister 1965-1974.

A MOJTAHED'S[7] WIFE WHO FOUNDED A GIRLS' SCHOOL

In those days so-called *mollá*s still claimed that sending girls to school was contrary to the law of Islam, but this view was not held by all the clergy.

Mrs. Safiyeh Yazdi was the wife of Aqá Sheykh Mohammad Hoseyn Yazdi, one of the five high-ranking *mojtahed*s who in the early years of the constitutional regime were chosen by the country's *mojtahed*s and *olamá* to sit in the Majles and make sure that projected legislation would not diverge from Islamic precepts. Aqá Sheykh Mohammad Hoseyn's accession to the rank of *mojtahed* was attested by Ákhund Kázem Khorásani of Najaf in Iraq, who was the generally recognized chief *mojtahed* of the Shi'ite Moslems at that time. To remove the doubts concerning girls' education, Sheykh Mohammad Hoseyn encouraged his wife to establish a girls' school, named the Effatiyeh School. This was opened in or around 1910 on Cyrus Avenue, Tehran.

Safiyeh Khánom was a high-minded and conscientious person. At her husband's request, she gave lectures on the status and rights of women in addition to the usual lessons, with the result that she was once warned by the Ministry of Education that no subjects outside the official syllabus should be taught to the pupils. Nevertheless, the influence of her husband—who was a truly religious man, open-minded, unpretentious, and brave—sufficed to ensure that her good work could continue. Sheykh Hoseyn gave his monthly 100-*tomán* parliamentary expense-allowance to the needy, wore garments of cheap cotton cloth, sat on a straw mat, and ate and drank very sparingly, abstaining even from tea. Safiyeh Khánom's action, coming from the wife of such a person, deeply impressed the masses, and agitations against her school therefore carried no weight.

from bondage—and not only to put up with words; for on one occasion some of them threw her into a pool of water. As a result, this brave lady was afflicted with leg trouble for the rest of her life.

In 1911 Mrs. Máh-Rokh Gowharshenás founded the Taraqqi Girls' School on Zahir ol-Eslám street, Tehran. The school, which later became a secondary school, attracted pupils from the adjacent section of the city and supplied an education which enabled many to win distinction. One was the eminent lawyer, Mrs. Qodsiyeh Hejázi, who writes about her late headmistress as follows:

> Máh-Rokh Khánom's life and character can best be described as holy. Indeed she was a model of the perfect woman. She took endless pains to achieve positive results. I myself am one of the beneficiaries of her care. She admitted me free of charge to the school and gave me valuable help in all sorts of ways. Although this noble-hearted and high-minded lady had not herself received any proper schooling, she came to know a great deal about the problems of education and the techniques of teaching. Her aim was to provide society with wives and mothers having good characters, ample skills, and wide knowledge. She paid more attention to the moral upbringing of her pupils than to any other matter.

Since Máh-Rokh Khánom's husband disapproved of her progressive activities, she was obliged to keep the fact that she was running a school hidden from him for two years. When the secret leaked out, her husband started beating his head and face with shame and then said to her, "How shall I reply to your father in the next world when he asks me why I did not restrain the daughter whom he had entrusted to me from carrying on a sinful antireligious activity and thus ruining his respectability?"

The Taraqqi Girls' School was so progressive that it admitted boys to the junior classes, where they and the girls sat and studied side by side; and it won such an honorable renown that a Moslem clergyman who had attained the rank of *mojtahed*,[8] namely Áqá Sheykh Ramazán Ali Khalili Eráqi, sent his daughter there. Since women teachers were hard to find, indeed virtually nonexistent, in those days, Mrs. Gowharshenás invited scholarly and reputable

The Constitutional Revolution and Women's Awakening

She was a well-dressed, well-spoken, and dignified woman. She had a daughter, Morassa' Khánom (afterward the wife of Mr. Háyeri Sháhbágh), who studied modern sciences and mathematics besides acquiring a good knowledge of music, and later also became a headmistress; and the latter's daughter Minádokht qualified as a doctor of medicine and is now a gynecologist. The Effatiyeh School became a secondary school and had some distinguished scholars on its teaching staff. Among them were Áqá Abu'l-Qásem Khán Neráqi, Mirzá Mohammad Khán Neráqi, Áqá Sheykh Ahmad Oshkuri, Mrs. Badr ol-Moluk Vasiqi, Mrs. Nosrat Taqvá, and Mrs. Mohtaram Lotfi. These men and women held enlightened views and were among the pioneers who contributed most to the spread of girls' education in Iran.

As this example shows, clear-sighted members of the Moslem clergy not only showed great devotion in the cause of constitutional government and national freedom for the whole people of Iran, but also gave pioneering help in the uplift of the nation's women. They too saw the need to strip the blinkers of ignorance off the women's eyes and to bring up a new generation of conscientious, educated mothers.

ANOTHER DEVOUTLY RELIGIOUS PIONEER

Born in 1872, Mrs. Máh-Rokh Gowharshenás was the daughter of Hájj Mirzá Ja'far and became the wife of Mirzá Mohammad Báqer, a merchant. She was strictly religious and devotedly humanitarian. At the time of the constitutional revolution, she was one of a group who pledged themselves on oath never to give up the struggle for women's rights, not even for a moment's pause and not even in the face of death or hardship or unhappiness. The special emblem which the members of the group designed for themselves and always wore was a signet ring engraved with two clasped hands. Along with other enlightened ladies, they played an important part in the demonstration outside the Majles and the boycott of foreign goods in 1911. Yet Máh-Rokh Khánom often had to put up with insulting and indecent words from the same poor Iranian women whom she was struggling to rescue male sympathizers with the cause of women's advancement to teach in the Taraqqi Girls' Secondary School. Among them were Mr. Mohammad Mehrán, who combined attendance as a student at the Dár ol-Fonun[9] with work as a teacher at this girls' school in the belief that he could thus contribute effectively to the spiritual uplift of his fellow citizens. Mrs. Máh-Rokh Gowharshenás's illustrious life ended in 1938.

THE TARBIAT GIRLS' SCHOOL AND THE CONSTITUTIONALIST LADY WHO FOUNDED IT

Máh-Soltán Amir-e Sehhi was born in 1877. Her father, who was an enlightened merchant, provided tuition at home for his daughters, and her husband Mirzá Asadolláh, who was a liberal-minded *mojtahed*,[10] personally took in hand her further education. During the struggle for constitutional government, she strongly sympathized with the constitutionalists and joined the group in Tehran who formed the National Ladies' Society. Along with the other members, she took part in the demonstration on 1 December 1911, carrying the banner "Independence or Death," and like the rest of them she pawned or sold her jewelry and collected money to help the patriotic volunteers. These ladies carried their zeal to the point of standing with their children on the tramway tracks, as a sign that they would rather die with their children than live in the slavery which would result from disregard of the nation's wishes.

Máh-Soltán Khánom decided to found a school after she had observed that the spread of literacy among women was a factor which helped to strengthen the constitutionalist movement. In taking this step, she exposed herself to all sorts of difficulties and antagonisms. The school was named the Tarbiat Girls' School. At that time there were only three or four other girls' schools in Tehran. The first problem was the unwillingness of landlords to lease a house for the school, which they imagined would be a center of corruption. After a house had been found and the landlord had been reassured, certain people in the locality began to stir up opposition and cause trouble. They several times removed the school signboard or threw stones at it. One of Máh-Soltán Khánom's bitter memories of the time when she headed the school is of the way in which these neighbors used to get loiterers—very often psychopaths who then prowled the streets as there were no lunatic asylums—to walk into the school's premises and grin at the terrified girls, while they themselves would gather outside the gateway to enjoy the spectacle and jeer. In reply to complaints from the school's governors, they stated that the best way to avoid further trouble would be to close this "den of iniquity" and let no more girls through its gate. On the anniversary of the Emám Hoseyn's martyrdom in the lunar month of Moharram, Máh-Soltán Khánom organized recitals at the school every year but had great difficulty in getting reciters and elegists.

In the Tarbiat School's curriculum, the number of hours assigned for the teaching of Islamic precepts was large. The intention was to prove for the masses that acquisition of knowledge is in no way incompatible with maintenance of belief in God. Since the government then gave no help or protection to private schools, the responsibility for the children's safety lay on the shoulders of the school's management alone. The only help and support ever received was from the parents, who were wholly sympathetic. Many a pupil's mother laid her domestic troubles before the kindly and understanding headmistress and sought advice. Even so, there were sometimes parents who dropped out and withdrew their daughters for fear of losing respectability or being accused of apostasy and other imaginary sins.

There were also grave financial difficulties. Not infrequently Máh-Soltán Khánom made good the school's losses from her own private resources. As time passed, however, the position improved, and the school was divided into primary and secondary sections. One of the founder's daughters, Mehrangiz Amir-e Sehhi, took over and is still carrying on the work begun by her mother.

THE OPINION OF A PIONEER

I am not so worried about the humiliations and subordination of women. In our country there have always been numerous women who dominated men and indirectly determined the course of important events. What distresses me is the fact that they gained this influence through charm and allurement, and felt no need for intelligence and rationality.

This opinion was expressed by Dorrat ol-Ma'áli Khánom, a pioneer of girls' education and a fearless patriot. During the Lesser Autocracy (June 1908-July 1909, when Mohammad Ali Sháh ruled autocratically after overthrowing the constitutional regime), she removed the veil from her face and twisted it round her neck, and boldly set out with other like-minded women to pursue practical goals by all possible means. She succeeded in founding the Dorrat ol-Madáres Girls' School at that time, and while rendering great services to education, she did not neglect other forms of social work. After her death, her daughters Shams ol-Nahár and Shams ol-Zohá carried on the school, which was renamed Ázarm School, for a number of years before transferring it to the Ministry of Education. It still exists. There is a photograph of Dorrat ol-Ma'áli Khánom in an album of the Ázarm High School which has been preserved in the government archives, but few people know whose photograph it is.

This lady, whom the authoress afterward had the privilege to meet and know, often used to speak as follows:

> Women, in their roles as mothers, wives or sweethearts, have much more influence and power over men than they suppose. Indeed, they often determine the fate of men. The minds and hearts of important men have usually been swayed by beloved wives. In this way women have a hand in dismissals and appointments and the management or mismanagement of state affairs. But what is the good of that, if they spend all their effort on learning how to allure and blandish and do not learn how to think clearly and judge soundly? It is this situation which makes them corruptible and unable either to find real happiness for themselves or to guide men on the road to good.

An incident related in the memoirs of Mokhber ol-Saltaneh (Hedáyat)[11] gives a good illustration of the influence and power which the women in the harems kept by the grandees used to exercise.

Náser ol-Din Sháh had given the post of governor general of Fárs to his brother Mohammad Taqi Mirzá Rokn ol-Dowleh, but after two or three months he decided to give it to someone else. When Rokn ol-Dowleh learned about this, he wrote a brief note to Náser ol-Din Sháh's favorite wife, Fátemeh Khánom Anis ol-Dowleh, asking her to help in the case and stop his dismissal. Anis ol-Dowleh then wrote a letter to the Sháh in these terms: "I would sacrifice my life for you, it is worth less than the blessed dust under your feet. Not long ago Rokn ol-Dowleh went to Fárs; why do you wish to dismiss him now? If a bigger prepayment is needed, he will pay it. If he is dismissed, your Majesty's subjects will be dismayed. They will ask why a governor who has scarcely arrived has to be sent back so soon. Please let the eunuch bring back your reply!" Náser ol-Din Sháh wrote at the foot of Anis ol-Dowleh's letter: "To Anis ol-Dowleh. Rokn ol-Dowleh will remain in Fárs. Nobody is going to replace him. No prepayment is needed."[12]

THE ROLE OF THE AMERICAN GIRLS' SCHOOL

In 1874 a group of American Christian missionaries who had been sent to Iran opened a school for boys and girls in Tehran. The girls' section was run by two high-minded ladies, Miss Radlett and Miss King. For a long time only Christian and foreign girls were admitted. Iranian parents were prevented by the obstacles and inhibitions which then obstructed women's (and Iran's) advancement from sending their daughters to the school for education. In 1890, however, Náser ol-Din Sháh expressed a desire to see this educational establishment. During his visit, he not only spoke encouraging words to the teachers and staff, but also asked whether there were any Iranian pupils. Despite their fear of incurring the royal displeasure, they had to reply that one Iranian pupil was attending the girls' school; and although they imagined the contrary, the sháh was inwardly glad to learn that an Iranian girl was there. A blackboard on which the sháh had written some words in chalk was suitably framed, glazed, and preserved.

With rare exceptions, however, this school did not admit Moslem pupils until after the introduction of constitutional government, when the first private schools for girls were founded and officially recognized. The first Moslem Iranian girls, who completed their studies at the American Girls' School in 1921, were Badr ol-Dojá (Mehr-Táj Rakhshán) and Maryam Ardalán. The latter was afterward for some time in charge of a girls' orphanage founded by Rezá Sháh. Perhaps a brief sketch of the school's later history will not be out of place in this chapter.

In 1940 the American Girls' School, then greatly expanded and having a large number of pupils, was transferred with all its equipment to the Iranian government following the nationalization of foreign schools in Iran; but after an interval of fifteen years it was revived as an English language-teaching institute with the name Iran-Bethel (later renamed Damávand High School).

During the period when the girls' school was administered by the American missionaries, about five hundred girls graduated and received its leaving certificate, which was endorsed by the head of New York State University. The school's first pupils to reach the American university's B.A. degree standard were Hurásá Fasá (Shokuh), Soghrá Ázarmi, Alexandra Rubián (an Armenian Iranian girl), and the late Akhtar Kalántari; this was in 1940.

One member of the American mission who made a particularly zealous effort for girls' education was Miss Jane Elizabeth Doolittle, who arrived in Iran in 1921 and served for forty-five years, including thirty-nine years (1927-1966) as head of the girls' school; she was asked to remain at her post when the Iranian Ministry of Education took over. Having come to love Iran as her second home, she chose to stay in the country after her retirement, and took charge of a clinic on Khánqáh Avenue which had been bought and was being financed by graduates of the American school. She still carries on this work. The opportunity to help sick and destitute women and their children is a joy to her. For her services to Iranian girls' education over so many years, the Ministry of Education honored Miss Doolittle with the Medal of Appreciation (First Class) in February 1972.

A magazine called *Women's Universe (Álam-e Nesván)* was started in 1921 by Mrs. Boyce and the school's Association of Graduates, with Mrs. Navvábeh Safavi as the responsible editor. It continued to be published for fourteen years and helped worthily to broaden women's mental horizons and impart better understanding of their domestic and social roles.

The Association of Graduates of the American Girls' School, which was founded in 1914, has devoted much effort to social services, including anti-illiteracy work. A literacy class for indigent adult women and girls was opened in 1946 under Miss Doolittle's direction. As already mentioned, she also manages a small clinic, at which two lady doctors who are members of the association treat indigent women and children free of charge. The association has a library, which was assembled in 1963 and has since then been gradually enlarged.

THE ECOLE FRANCO-PERSANE

Another institution which arose during the struggle for constitutional government was the Ecole Franco-Persane. This school's founder, Yusof Khán Mo'addeb ol-Molk, was later to play an important part in the history of Iranian girls' education, and the school itself was to become the nucleus of a more important institution.

Mirzá Yusof Khán Mo'addeb ol-Molk Rishár (Richard) was the son of a Frenchman employed as a professor at the Dár ol-Fonun[13] and of an Iranian mother. Both parents were Moslems. He himself also taught at the Dár ol-Fonun. As soon as his two daughters, Emily Khánom Neshát ol-Saltaneh and Qamar Khánom Neshát ol-Dowleh, were of an age to be educated, he tried to arrange adequate home tuition for them but found that the cost of hiring the competent tutors who would be needed for the various subjects was too heavy to be borne by one man. It would be better, he thought, to organize larger classes. He discussed his idea with some prominent men of the time, who were friendly with him and anxious to give their daughters a good education, and they eagerly welcomed it. Eventually the well-planned classes were started in a private house in 1906.

The number of entrants gradually rose, and the range of the classes was extended until finally they took the shape of a school. Mo'addeb ol-Molk provided a chemistry and physics laboratory and introduced a very thorough practical method of French teaching. A well-equipped and well-organized school working on sound educational principles thus came into being. Its cultured and patriotic founder assumed the role of headmaster.

Mo'addeb ol-Molk personally told the authoress about some of the many harrassments to which he was subjected in his efforts to keep the school going. For instance, when the school began to expand and win a reputation, a certain influential *mollá* (whose name the authoress prefers not to mention) mounted the pulpit and wrathfully declared to his congregation that "a house on such-and-such street has fallen into the hands of an Armenian, who is using it as a so-called school where he lures Moslem girls by pretending to give them lessons and leads their minds astray and turns them into unbelievers and wantons." At the end of his long tirade, the *mollá* promised his hearers terrestrial and celestial recompense if they would equip themselves with spades and pickaxes and then follow him and bring that nest of corruption down onto the heads of its inmates. Fearing a mass attack and danger to the lives of the girls, Mo'addeb ol-Molk hoisted the French flag over the house and got the French to post one of their legation guards in front of it, as signs that the place was under French protection. He hoped that this would suffice to deter his adversaries from causing harm; but the dignitaries and notables whose daughters had been attending the school were so much under the thumb of the *mollá*s, and so terrified of being denounced as infidels or of seeing their daughters molested in the streets, that they stopped the girls from coming. As a result the school was almost brought to a standstill. Mo'addeb ol-Molk in his predicament consulted certain parents and guardians who were well versed in contemporary ways, and they devised a plan. They sent a messenger to the unfriendly *mollá* and provided the wherewithal to placate his wrath. Immediately—in his sermon on the following day—he brought up the matter of the Ecole Franco-Persane. He had not made adequate inquiries, he declared, as he now knew that the man had given up Christianity and been honored by reception into Islam and should therefore be treated with affection and respect. Moreover, he had learned that the man gave lessons on the Qor'án and the religious laws and was propagating Islam in the school. He therefore now advised that the man be treated with affection and respect. He regretted his mistake and stated that no hostile action would be taken against that meritorious educational institution. After this, Mo'addeb ol-Molk restored the school to normalcy and ran it without further anxiety.

NOTES

1. The Fundamental Law of 30 December 1906 and the Supplementary Fundamental Law of 30 September 1907.
2. Anjoman-e Ázádi-ye Zanán.
3. Anjoman-e Mokhaddarát-e Vatan.
4. Prime Minister, October 1909-July 1910 and March-July 1911.
5. These paragraphs were contributed by Mrs. Zeynab Amin.
6. Founder of the first modern private Iranian school (for boys) at Tabriz in 1896.
7. A Shi'ite Moslem clergyman of the highest rank. The criteria for attainment to this rank are outstanding merits in scholarship, piety and administrative ability, and these are assessed by consensus of the existing *mojtahed*s at the candidate's theological college. (At the important theological college at Qom, assessment on the basis of university-type study programs and examinations was introduced by the late Áyatolláh Borujerdi, but the practice has been dropped since his death in 1961.) A *mojtahed* may issue new rulings instead of following precedents. Every lesser clergyman must follow a living *mojtahed*.
8. See note 7.
9. Iran's first college of modern higher learning, founded in 1851 by the reforming minister Amir-e Kabir (who was put to death in 1852). Its first head was the writer and historian Rezá Qoli Hedáyat, and its first foreign teachers were mostly Austrian. The tuition was given in Persian and French.
10. See note 7.
11. Prime minister, 1928-1934. Prominent in the struggle for constitutional government and in the First World War. A pioneer of the movement for industrialization in Iran.
12. Anis ol-Dowleh's letter and Náser ol-Din Sháh's reply are reproduced in facsimile in Mokhber ol-Saltaneh's book, *Kháterát va Khatarát* (Tehran, 1329/1950).
13. See note 9.

IV

AFTER THE FIRST WORLD WAR

THE REUNIFICATION AND MODERNIZATION OF IRAN UNDER REZÁ SHÁH THE GREAT

During the First World War, Iran was neutral but not strong enough to prevent Russian, Turkish, German and British troops from fighting on her soil. The people suffered severely, and the government lost control of several parts of the country. The cabinet of Vosuq ol-Dowleh (1918-1919) did some useful preliminary work in the fields of education and public health, but was unable to restore order and national unity. This task fell to Rezá Khán Sardár-e Sepáh, who became commander-in-chief on 21 February 1921 and war minister also on 25 April 1921, prime minister on 28 October 1923, and then, by a constitutional amendment, the first Sháhansháh of the Pahlavi dynasty on 12 December 1925. His achievements in uniting and modernizing the country and enforcing fundamental reforms have given him an honored place in history as Rezá Sháh the Great.

Far from overlooking the hitherto-forgotten partners of Iranian men, he was always aware that the women would be an essential factor in the upbringing of an efficient new generation. He also knew that with their intelligence and perception they could provide valuable help in getting the creaky wheels of Iranian society on the move and in modifying obstructive and self-seeking attitudes prevalent among the men. From the start he showed sympathy for the women's cause in practical ways, but it was only after ten years on the throne that he judged the time ripe for the bold steps, described in the next chapter, which were to lay the foundation of women's rights and freedom in Iran.

Growing numbers of ministers, editors, writers, and the like were also sympathetic to the women's cause. The poets Iraj (1874-

1925), Áref (1882-1932) and Eshqi (1893-1924) swayed many minds with their deeply moving verses.[1]

The first state schools for girls were founded in 1918, and in the following years, particularly after the change of dynasty, their number grew at a rapid though inadequate pace. Private schools also increased in number and size and made a big contribution.[2] Employment opportunities for women grew less rapidly. They could get work as teachers, but not as officials or as secretaries.[3]

Change in the social environment was slow. Most of the people were stuck in the rut of old notions and habits, and many were susceptible to obscurantist preachings. The growing number of enlightened families were generally cautious of getting out of step with their neighbors: they were eager enough to send their daughters to school, but not bold enough to think of allowing them to work, let alone unveil.

Thus the problem in the postwar years was still primarily educational. If Iranian women were to attain a higher and juster status, it was necessary to spread knowledge and common sense among them, and among the men too, through schools, adult classes, and the press. There was also a pressing need for the teaching of hygiene, child care, and household management to Iranian women at that time.

These tasks were voluntarily and energetically undertaken by the Patriotic Women's League, which came into being at Tehran in 1922 and lasted until 1932, and by other devoted women in some of the provincial cities. Much of this chapter will be concerned with the activities of the league and of some of its leading members. The authoress wishes, however, first to record the sad case of a pioneer for whom the unpleasantness of the then existing environment finally became unbearable, and to describe the foundation and early life of Iran's first Women's Teacher Training College.

THE TRAGEDY OF A HEADMISTRESS AND ARTIST

Two well-educated sisters had sprung up like wild roses to grace the contemporary garden of Iranian education. The elder was named Muchul Várasteh, the younger became Mrs. Nosrat

Mostaghni. In or around the year 1915 they founded the Shams ol-Madáres Secondary School in Tehran. Their reputation as high-principled persons, their intrinsic ability, and their close supervision of the teaching and training of the schoolgirls drew the attention of prominent families to their school and enabled them to render great services to the cause of girls' education. They sympathized with the nationalist democrats and did their utmost to inspire the girls with a sense of patriotic duty and a willingness to help through social service.

Nosrat Khánom not only had a complete mastery of French, but like her brother Eskandar Khán was also an excellent painter; they were both pupils of Kamál ol-Molk, the great Iranian artist of the late nineteenth and early twentieth centuries. She was accomplished in water colors, oil paintings, miniatures, and silk embroideries. Some of her work was shown in an exhibition at the Takiye-ye Dowlat,[4] which was visited by the prime minister, Rezá Khán Sardár-e Sepáh, who expressed special interest in the work of this talented woman artist.

Unfortunately, no specimen of Nosrat Khánom's paintings, which have great monetary value as well as artistic merit, now remains in Iran. Her art did not gain due recognition in her own country.

Nosrat Khánom wore the veil and practiced the religion strictly. She knew the true measure of her abilities, but like most artists was very sensitive, even touchy. Not surprisingly, the unpleasantnesses and difficulties which she encountered—and which every Iranian woman who trod the new path and took up social work or teaching then had to face—deeply wounded her self-respect and finally made her lose heart. She gave up her work and lived the rest of her life as a recluse. Pain inflicted by the hostile environment and, above all, by an unhappy family affair which greatly distressed her, reduced this brilliant young woman artist and educationist to a state of worry and depression in which her hopes and ambitions soon faded. She refused to marry, and cut herself off from her friends and acquaintances.

After she had accustomed herself to solitude, her vitality ebbed and her face seemed to become shrouded in a dust of pessimism and despair. She sent her paintings and embroideries to her brother, who lived abroad. After the death of her only sister, she lived completely alone and shrank from meeting even her former pupils.

Her body was found in her room several hours after she had closed her eyes to this world and found release from its torments.

THE FIRST OFFICIAL HELP FOR GIRLS' EDUCATION

A small announcement in the newspapers in 1918 startled readers by revealing that the Ministry of Education, *Vaqfs*[5] and Fine Arts (as it was then called) had rubbed its sleepy eyes and cast a sympathetic glance at the country's girls. It had decided to found a Women's Teacher Training College and ten girls' primary schools, and to establish a Department of Public Instruction for Women. By that time, a decade has passed since the foundation of the first private girls' schools by liberal-minded and patriotic women, but not a single girls' school had yet been founded by by the government. The prime minister at the time was Vosuq ol-Dowleh, and the minister of education was Nasir ol-Dowleh (Ahmad Báder Khán).

After taking the decision, Nasir ol-Dowleh had to find staff and premises. For the two posts of head of the new department and director of the new training college, his choice fell on Mo'addeb ol-Molk Rishár, in view of the latter's experience and proved competence as founder and headmaster of the Ecole Franco-Persane (described in the previous chapter); and for the accommodation of the new training college, room was made available in the Ecole Franco-Persane's premises near the Yusofábád Avenue-Paris Avenue crossroads in Tehran.

THE WOMEN'S TEACHER TRAINING COLLEGE[6]

In status the Women's Teacher Training College was a secondary school, open to girls with the primary education certificate, but only going up to grade nine, which was as far as girls were thought able to reach in those days. Besides the usual subjects, principles of education and methods of teaching were studied.

After the First World War

In the first year of the college's existence, thirty pupils were admitted. Girls' school teachers also met in the college hall once a week for lessons in teaching methods. The courses on education were given by Mo'addeb ol-Molk himself together with the late Mr. Fázel, who held the title Fasih ol-Molk. Mr. Fázel was blind. He was a good scholar of French and Arabic and knew the Qor'án by heart. His lessons, and generally his presence, were a great help. As a result of his misfortune, he was employed throughout his career as a teacher in girls' secondary schools, because the girls (who wore the *chádor*) were spared the inconvenience of having to cover their faces while attending his classes. All the Iranian instructors appointed to the Women's Teacher Training College were elderly—and very learned—men; e.g., Dr. Mahmud Khán (chemistry), Mirzá Asadolláh Khán (mathematics), Fázel Farjád (Persian literature), Gholám Rezá Khán (calligraphy). A French lady, however, was responsible for the French teaching. Mo'addeb ol-Molk personally guided and supervised all the tuition and training. Two brilliant former pupils of the Ecole Franco-Persane, by name Fasá and Fasih ol-Moluk Mahámm, became the college's first graduates (*diplomées*), and were both later appointed inspectresses of girls' schools. Although the college, like other girls' secondary schools at that time, only offered a three-year course (i.e., up to grade nine), it was a full and heavy program requiring very hard work by the eager pupils to keep up with all the component subjects. Moreover, they worked under the close supervision of the strict and scholarly, though sympathetic, director and did practical training as well as academic study.

At the end of the college's third year, a celebration was held. The Ministry of Education sent two copies of the Holy Qor'án, which were presented to the third-year and first-year girls who had won the highest marks; they were Badr ol-Moluk[7] and Hormat Sepánlu, respectively. The ministry's gesture was seen as a great success for girls' schools in general.

In 1921, the Women's Teacher Training College was separated from the Ecole Franco-Persane, and Fasih ol-Moluk Mahámm was appointed head of the college. She was succeeded by Mr. Hojjat, a scholar of theology and the classics. In 1924 the Ministry of Education showed more interest in the college, and Dr. Isá Sadiq, who was then director general of education, selected a French lady, Mme. Hélène Hess, to be its next head. She was efficient and knowledgeable, and she brought about important changes and reforms in the curriculum and methods. The study of domestic science, child psychology, and better teaching methods was introduced, and particular attention was given to training through practical experience. Mme. Hess herself took on the teaching of pedagogic subjects for which there were no Iranian antecedents or textbooks. She wrote notes in French which were translated into Persian. Her notes on domestic science and on etiquette and morals were entrusted to the authoress (Mrs. Bámdád), who was then working at the college as a translator and supervisor. This enabled Mrs. Bámdád to compile the first Persian books on those subjects and then to get them printed[8] and supplied to secondary schools.

The Women's Teacher Training College was now flourishing and attracting the interest of many families. Later its course was extended from three to five years, and so was the course in all girls' secondary schools, whereas the course in boys' secondary schools lasted six years. One consequence of this discrepancy was that when the Higher Teacher Training College and other university faculties complied with Rezá Sháh the Great's wish that women should be admitted, a special preparatory course for female candidates had to be instituted at the Higher Teacher Training College so that they might cover the lost ground; otherwise, girls who had received their schooling under the old system would have been debarred. A special examination was held for women who had gained additional knowledge and experience after their completion of the original three-year or subsequent five-year teacher-training course or the five-year secondary-school course, e.g., by covering further ground with private tutors or by working as teachers; and the candidates who passed the examination were admitted to the university.[9] This was done with the sanction of the High Council of Education.

After the departure of Mme. Hess, Mrs. Hájar Tarbiat[10] was chosen to be the next head of the Women's Teacher Training College. In 1934 it was renamed Preliminary Teacher Training College for girls,[11] and Mr. Momtáz was appointed head.

SELF-DEFENSE BY COLLEGE GIRLS

Not long after the foundation of the Women's Teacher Training College, when the girls had eagerly and zealously got down to their studies and each was forming an ambition for the future, they suddenly received a report that at a mourning assembly (on one of the ten days of the anniversary of the Emám Hoseyn's martyrdom) an influential man of reactionary views had vehemently denounced the college and criticized girls' education in general, and had then urged his simple-minded hearers to attack and forcibly close all girls' schools.

One day when a group of girls from the college (one of whom was the authoress) were walking home, they encountered this person in a lonely street. After a whispered discussion of tactics, they advanced and hemmed him in on the sidewalk. Then one of the girls addressed him as follows: "We are fighting women, and our war is for freedom. We have large numbers of troops. By speaking to the common people as you did, you have endangered your life. We are going to take our revenge." The threat scared him much more than the girls had expected and to such an extent that he could only stammer in reply. First he begged for mercy, and then he promised never to say such things again if they would let him go.

Although it was learned that at the following day's mourning assembly he plaintively claimed to have been threatened with death by a large crowd of pistol-carrying women who had burst into his home, he nevertheless kept his promise and refrained from further troublemaking. Even so, the students of the college usually found their homeward routes obstructed by louts and street urchins, who shouted obscene words or scurrilous verses at them. On several occasions the girls beat these youths on the head with thick books which they pulled out from under their *chádor*s.

STEPS TO IMPROVE MIDWIFERY

Two years after the establishment of the Women's Teacher Training College, the same minister of education, Nasir ol-Dowleh, sent two of its students to study midwifery at the Tehrán Women's Hospital under the supervision of a French lady doctor, Mme. Fraschina; and this led eventually to the government's decision in 1930 to establish Iran's first School of Midwifery. Until then the conditions in which Iranian women gave birth had been deplorable. The old-fashioned midwives were illiterate and ignorant. Mothers frequently died of hemorrhages or infections caused by dirty hands and hygienically unclean instruments. The common people attributed this high mortality to a demon called the *Ál*, which lay in ambush for every mother who had just given birth and immediately snatched her away if she was left alone for a moment. For protection against this danger, the people had recourse to magic and talismans; e.g., it was thought that the placing of a skewer with onions on it above the mother's head would ward off the *Ál*.

The annual number of qualified midwives graduating from this school was at first only ten, which was, of course, inadequate; but greater attention was henceforth given to this vital matter, and training facilities were gradually extended.

MOHTARAM ESKANDARI AND THE FOUNDATION OF THE PATRIOTIC WOMEN'S LEAGUE

Mohtaram Eskandari (b. 1895) was the daughter of a Qájár prince, who afterward took the name Mohammad Ali Mirzá Eskandari. After studying under her father, she later perfected her knowledge of history, literature, and French under Mirzá Ali Mohammad Khán Mohaqqeqi, and eventually the pupil and the teacher became husband and wife. Her father was a militant adversary of despotism and one of the enlightened group who founded the Ádamiyat (Humanitarian) Society several years before the constitutional revolution. Among the society's active members were two other princes who were forerunners of the constitutionalist movement, Soleymán Mirzá and Yahyá Mirzá. From her early childhood onward, Mohtaram Khánom joined in conversations with her father's associates and especially with Mirzá Táher Tonákábuni, and among the subjects which they discussed were the disabilities of women. She thus acquired a restless and passionate turn of mind. Before the start of the struggle for constitutional government, the Ádamiyat Society (which was secret) had been unmasked and dissolved; but after the grant of the constitution it was reestablished as the Hoquq (Civil Rights) Society, and began to issue a periodical, also named *Hoquq,* in which questions of women's rights were often discussed. This was suspended during the "short autocracy" of Mohammad Ali Sháh (June 1908-July 1909). After the victory of the constitutionalist forces, Mohtaram Khánom, who had cherished overconfident hopes that the constitutional revolution would bring recognition of women's rights, soon observed how little attention was being given to the matter.

The fact that great postwar changes abroad were making no difference to women's status in Iran disappointed Mohtaram Khánom even more and convinced her that it was her duty to intervene directly in the struggle. She contacted a small number of other freedom-seeking women, and in 1922 they formed a society which they named the Patriotic Women's League.[12] She was elected president, and in spite of much suffering from a slipped vertebral disc which caused her to walk with a stoop, she carried on her task with the utmost energy and bravery. The other ladies on the league's executive committee were all equally courageous and devoted. Their great services cannot be fully appreciated without a knowledge of conditions in Iran at that time, when women were not allowed any sort of self-expression but were required to obey their fathers, husbands, and even distant male relatives unquestioningly. Among the league's leading members were Nur ol-Hodá Manganeh, Fakhr-e Áfáq Pársá, Fakhr-e Ozmá Arghun (Ádel), Mastureh Afshár, and Safiyeh Eskandari.

The aims of the league, according to its articles of association (which have been preserved), were to emphasize continuing respect for the laws and rituals of Islam, to promote the education and moral upbringing of girls, to encourage national industries, to spread literacy among adult women, to provide care for orphaned girls, to set up hospitals for poor women, to organize cooperative societies as a means of developing national industries, and to give material and moral support to the country's defenders in the event of war. In article seventeen, the league affirmed that in matters explicitly concerning it, but depending on governmental help, it had the duty of taking action, directly or by means of newspaper articles and leaflets, to obtain attention and help from the authorities.

In 1923 the league published a periodical named *Nesván-e Vatankhwáh (Patriotic Women)* and started classes for adult women. At gatherings of women and girls, even at private parties and school celebrations, members of the league made fervent speeches encouraging their hearers to demand legitimate rights. In the hope of drawing attention to the problems, and indeed to the existence, of women, Mohtaram Khánom and her colleagues in the league sometimes did things which were meant to cause commotion, such as the burning of copies of a pamphlet on women's wiles in the Meydán-e Tupkháneh (the present Meydán-e Sepáh), where newspaper boys were offering it for sale to the accompaniment of shouted ribaldries. Mohtaram and the other ladies each collected a number of copies, which they then set alight in the middle of the square. In the ensuing tumult they were dragged to the police station, where Mohtaram made good use of the occasion for propaganda. "We did it," she said, "to defend the honor of your mothers and sisters. We are rational and intelligent like all human beings, but we are not wily." Her impassioned and impressive words moved the police officers so much that they took her side. In later years she worked, despite her infirmity, as headmistress of a state girls' school. Other actions and experiences of the Patriotic Women's League will be recounted in biographical sketches of some of its members.

This brave woman entered a hospital in 1924 for an operation on her spine, which she did not survive. Alas, she closed her eyes before reaching the age of thirty and without seeing the fulfillment of her great aspirations.

THE LEAGUE'S SECOND PRESIDENT

The league's members chose a person with long experience of conditions abroad to be their second president. Mastureh Afshár's father, Majd ol-Saltaneh Afshár, was a distinguished and courageous reformist resident at Rezá'ieh (formerly Orumieh) in Ázarbáiján; and her mother's father, Emám Qoli Malek-Qásemi, was an influential and patriotic notable of the same province. In addition to Persian, she knew Russian and Turkish and also French very well, having learned them during long stays at Tiflis and Istanbul in her youth. From then onward, she devoted her life to the uplift of Iran's socially retarded women. In her efforts, after her return to her beloved homeland, for the cause of women's awakening and women's rights, she made good use of the observations which she had accumulated while living abroad. She showed such energy and strength of purpose in her work for the Patriotic Women's League that after Mohtaram Eskandari's death she was elected president. With the help of the members, she kept the league's organization in being and worked hard in all its activities, such as the arrangement and giving of lectures and adult classes and the writing of newspaper articles. Her knowledge of the advances made in other countries was very useful, as it helped her to persuade a number (admittedly no more than a handful) of the leading men that women and mothers must be given a proper place in society. One objective for which she showed special concern was to convince families of the propriety of sending their daughters to the few schools which had been set up with so much trouble to make literacy accessible to girls. Fortunately, her advice gained a measure of acceptance, thanks to the potency of her pen.

THE LEAGUE'S SECRETARY AND ADULT-CLASS ORGANIZER; ITS FIRST THEATRICAL SHOW

An important role in the league was played by its secretary. Nur ol-Hodá Manganeh was an accomplished writer, talented poet, and skillful calligrapher; she also had a good knowledge of French. She was one of the daughters of a revenue official, Ali

Mirzá Moshir-e Daftar. Thanks to her father's keen concern for the education of his daughters, she was highly cultured, and she resolved to use her knowledge and artistic abilities in pursuit of the goals of cultural development and human rights for Iranian women—goals shared by all the members of the Patriotic Women's League, who chose her to be its first secretary. She was a forceful and frequent contributor to its periodical *Nesván-e Vatankhwáh*, which came out in 1923 after the grant of a publication license to Princess Moluk Eskandari. In addition to this, she wrote numerous articles for newspapers and periodicals then in wide circulation, such as the newspaper *Setáre-ye Irán* and the periodicals *Zabán-e Zanán* (edited by Sadiqeh Dowlatábádi), *Bánuván* (edited by Fakhr-e Ozmá Arghun), and at a later time *Zan-e Emruz* (edited by Badr ol-Moluk Bámdád). Two themes which she particularly emphasized in her articles were the importance of using Iran-made goods and of women's participation in social work.

It was on her suggestion that the Patriotic Women's League decided to give literacy classes for adult women. At the same time the league decided to kill two birds with one stone by organizing a theatrical performance which would raise funds for the launching of the adult classes and the magazine *Nesván-e Vatankhwáh* and would moreover provide entertainment for house-bound women. The courageous Nur ol-Hodá Khánom offered her own home, which was large and fairly suitable. Invitation cards for the play, which was called *Wedding Reception (Jashn-e Arusi)*, were printed and then sold by members to their acquaintances. It must be borne in mind that in those days only men were admitted to cinemas and stage shows, both forms of entertainment being barred to women. For the date of the performance, an evening in the daytime-fasting month of Ramazán was chosen, namely 27 Ramazán 1342 (3 May 1924), because in Ramazán women were allowed to go out into the streets during the first watch of the night; at other times of year, custom required them to "take the sun home," i.e., not be out of doors after sunset. In this first women's play, the stage was illuminated by means of paraffin lamps and chandeliers. The audience amounted to about three hundred women, mostly from prominent families, who, of course, all came wearing black *chádor*s and veils; and the cast also consisted entirely of women. The talented Armenian Iranian actress Varto Tarián (whose daughter is today a university professor) was the producer and principal player in the role of the bride. Nur ol-Hodá Khánom had previously obtained secretly a permit for the gathering from the police.

The first act of the play went successfully, and the spectators were absorbed in enjoyment of the second act, when suddenly knocks on the front door were heard. A squad of policemen had come, bringing an order from their headquarters to disperse the gathering immediately. Dreadful dangers now surrounded the ladies; they could expect to be disgraced, to be interrogated by their husbands, to see their families vilified by guttersnipes. Mohtaram Eskandari calmed them down, and members of the league's committee directed their departure. They escaped through side doors and over the flat roofs of the neighboring houses. Nur ol-Hodá and some of the committee members then took the actresses playing the bride's and bridegroom's parts into the drawing room and opened the front door for the policemen to enter. It was a wedding celebration, she told them. Mrs. Varto Tarián, in recalling the incident, is full of praise for the sangfroid with which the committee members, and in particular Mohtaram Eskandari, handled this grim situation.

That was by no means the end of the affair. In the following days the local ruffians, and the ragamuffin children who at that time lacked any occupation or recreation and could insult women without fear of any chastisement, amused themselves and tormented the organizers of the play by incessantly shouting foul abuse and by throwing stones and sticks at anybody who came out of Nur ol-Hodá's house. On one day a gang of ruffians and loafers egged on by so-called *mollá*s broke into the house and gave Nur ol-Hodá a severe beating and looted her furniture and belongings, thereby causing her heavy loss. The lack of protection against the threats to her life obliged her to move temporarily to another abode, and the physical and mental ordeal made her ill for a while. Yet her purpose had been achieved; for the adult classes were duly launched with the proceeds of the sale of tickets for the play. Moreover, it was not long before the resolute members of the Patriotic Women's League managed to hold three successive cinema evenings in a house in another part of the city. In retrospect, it seems amazing that a plan to impart literacy to a quite small number of adult women should have required such suffering and such courage; but anyone who remembers the shape of things in those days will appreciate the self-sacrifice of Nur ol-Hodá Manganeh and her colleagues.

She helped in the adult classes and was an active member of all the league's committees. To her fearless practical work for the cause, she added the composition and publication of books for the guidance of young women: *Ráhámuz-e Khánvádeh (Guide to Family Life), Dust-e Shomá (Your Friend), Sahnehá-ye Zendegi (Scenes from Daily Life), Pandámuz (Maxims to Remember), Náqus (The Bell), Fánus (The Lantern), Ádáb-e Mo'ásharat va Tadbir-e Manzil (Domestic Economy and Etiquette), Diván-e Ash'ār (Collected Poems), Tagarg (Hail), Golgasht (Rose Garden),* and another collection of poems on ethical and social subjects called *Banafsheh (Violets)*, which was published in 1968. In 1955 she edited and published a monthly magazine called *Bibi (Lady)*, which dealt with scholarly matters and literary criticism.

Through such tireless efforts by a small number of pioneers, the ground was gradually prepared for the future upsurge of Iran's women. When their long-cherished hopes were fulfilled, a substantial group of enlightened women were ready to step forward and quickly occupy worthy positions in society.

THE FIRST TEACHER OF THE ADULT CLASS

The first teacher of the adult class was a member of the executive committee of the Patriotic Women's League, Mrs. Nosrat Moshiri. She had received her initial education from her father, Mirzá Áqá Khán Esfaháni, a liberal who was prominent in preconstitutional days and lived at Tabriz. It was her father who inspired her patriotism and devotion to freedom. She had also pursued further studies under the guidance of a learned scholar named Yahyavi. When the league started its literacy class for adult

After the First World War

women, she volunteered to serve as the teacher. One of her delightful memories is of teaching an elderly lady to read and write. This lady's daughter and daughter-in-law had been attending the adult class for some time, and when her son went away on a journey she too joined the class so that she might learn how to write letters to him and read his letters without an intermediary. She set to work with such zeal and assiduity that she succeeded in making herself literate in a short time. One day she came in great haste to her teacher to express thanks. With tears of joy in her eyes, she kissed Mrs. Moshiri and told the good news that she had been able to read a letter from her son all by herself without having to request a favor from her daughter or her daughter-in-law. "What more precious reward could I have had," asked Mrs. Moshiri, "than that old lady's happy tears?"

Mrs. Moshiri believes that one of the worst consequences of veiling was that it exposed respectable women to danger from slander. Not infrequently women of bad character played vile tricks on other women in pursuit of advancement for themselves. For example, with the help of marriage brokeresses who had access to particular houses, they would make their way into the presence of wealthy men and get lavish gifts from them by pretending that they were the reputedly beautiful and charming female members of well-known families. Naturally, such dishonesty and perfidy often gave rise to nasty incidents.

Mrs. Moshiri said that the Patriotic Women's League sought and obtained advice from distinguished liberal-minded men, among whom she mentioned Seyyed Hasan Taqizádeh, Sa'id Nafisi, Ebráhim Khwajeh Nuri, and Dr. Rezázádeh Shafaq. She gave the following particulars of the league's officers: president, Mohtaram Eskandari and after her death Mastureh Afshár; vice-president, Princess Moluk Eskandari (who held the license to publish the league's magazine *Nesván-e Vatankhwáh*); first secretary, Nur ol-Hodá Manganeh (who was also the principal writer for the magazine); teacher of the adult class, Mrs. Nosrat Moshiri; second secretary, Mrs. Sharifi; inspector, Abbáseh Páyevar; inspector, Malekeh Abu'l-Fathzádeh; other members of the executive committee, Kobrá Janáni, Princess Eskandari, Tubá Baqa'i, Effat ol-

Moluk Khwájeh Nuri, Nazm ol-Moluk Khwájeh Nuri, Fakhr-e Ozmá Arghun, Háyedeh Moqbel, Turán Afshár, Akhtar ol-Saltaneh Siádat, Ásaf ol-Moluk, Akhtar ol-Saltaneh Foruhar, Eshrat ol-Zamán Ásaf, and several others.

ANOTHER MEMBER WHO WAS A TEACHER, JOURNALIST AND POETESS

One of the most energetic members of the league's executive committee was Fakhr-e Ozmá Arghun, who had literary talents. She was once moved to write a fiery patriotic poem with a verse saying that "the blood of traitors must be shed, and stain Iran's soil tulip-red." It was published in a newspaper named *Eqdám (Action),* which came out in 1923-1924. The poem shaped her destiny because it led to her acquaintance and marriage with the newspaper's editor, the journalist and novelist Abbás Khalili.

Fakhr-e Ozmá Khánom, whom many will remember under her later name Fakhr-e Ádel Khal'atbari, was born at Tehran in 1899. Her father, Mokrem ol-Soltán, was one of the well-educated army officers of the time and held the rank of general in command of a division (then called *Amir-e Tomán*). From childhood to adulthood she studied at home under her father's supervision, receiving lessons in Persian and Arabic literature, Islamic law and theology, history, astronomy, and French from well-qualified teachers. She succeeded in obtaining an official certificate of competence in French from the Institut Franco-Persan. Afterward she applied herself to the study of English at the American school. At that time the number of Iranian women who knew French almost as well as their mother tongue could be counted on the fingertips. She was also well versed in music and proficient in painting and embroidery, though in her later life she ceased to take much interest in any art except poetry. She began by composing songs, and then developed a predilection for social and revolutionary verse. Her marriage to Mr. Khalili only lasted a few years, but they had a daughter who has become famous today as the eloquent and graceful poetess Simin Behbeháni.

Fakhr-e Ozmá joined the Patriotic Women's League in her

After the First World War

young days and was an energetic champion of women's causes. In collaboration with her second husband, she published the newspaper *Áyande-ye Irán (The Future of Iran)*, and in 1932 she took over its editorship. A little later she launched the periodical *Bánuván (Ladies)*, which she personally edited. She was one of the active members of the Ladies' Center. The authoress (Mrs. Bámdád) worked with her at the Ladies' Center and the Women's Teacher Training College, and they became good friends.

Throughout her working life, Fakhr-e Ozmá Khánom taught French in Tehran secondary schools and devoted herself to girls' education. She founded and was for a long time headmistress of the Dabirestán-e Bánuván, a school providing secondary education for adult women. After the Second World War, she was active for a time in the Democrat Party of Iran. Ill health obliged her to retire from the service of the Ministry of Education, and she spent the last eight years of her life with her children in Washington. In accordance with her will, her remains were sent to Iran for burial in the mother country which she had served so well.

She had expressed her wish that this be done in two verses which reflect her devoted patriotism:

> My country! Both my body and my soul
> I happily will sacrifice for you.
> And I request my loving friends to wrap
> my body in your flag when I am dead!

Each of the four children whom she left has inherited her taste and talent for poetry.

The following is a good example of her art:

"A Woman's Beauty"

> A woman's beauty is not to be found
> in curls or rosy cheeks or budlike lips,
> or satin skirt or dress of crêpe georgette,
> or patent-leather shoes or pleated blouse.
> Truly her beauty lies in excellence
> of character and mind. Then, candlelike,
> her presence brightens every gathering.

> O zephyr, waft these questions to the men!
> Why in this country do you call us "weak"?
> If we are weak, then why have we been charged
> to breed a Rostamlike[13] stouthearted breed?
> Dear women, strive to dress yourselves in robes
> of knowledge! That dress will give most delight.
> It is so beautiful that, like Farhád,[14]
> you ought to strive for it all through your life.

THE WEAPON OF THE PEN

Another leading member of the league also wielded the weapon of the pen with great effect. Homá Mahmudi was an eloquent writer and poet, with a restless temperament. Whenever there was a possibility of getting articles in favor of women's freedom published in the newspapers and periodicals of those days, her fervent contributions made a deep impression. She also several times appeared on the stage in plays put on by Kamál ol-Vezáreh Mahmudi. She had been one of the leaders of the women's demonstrations outside the Majles at the time of the Russian ultimatum in 1911. Many of her articles were printed in the magazine *Álam-e Nesván (Women's Universe)*, which was run by the graduates of the American Girls' School.

The best way to give the reader an idea of Homá Khánom's revolutionary and patriotic spirit will be to quote some examples of her poetry. In regard to the first piece, it must be explained that the late Dabir-e A'zam Bahrámi had written a series of newspaper articles, which he signed with the pen name F. Barzgar, cruelly mocking and reproaching Iran's veiled and illiterate women. This was his way of explaining and condemning the harm to Iranian families (and the nation) when their upbringing and behavior remained in the hands of ignorant women. Dabir-e A'zam's article caused intense resentment among certain women and stirred them to reply. The resultant controversy attracted public attention to the disastrous results of the backwardness of Iranian women. In Homá Mahmudi's retorts to F. Barzgar (which means "farmer"), the wording of her verses shows how her passion for freedom had reached the bursting point.

"Homá Mahmudi's Reply to F. Barzgar"
(in the newspaper Irán, 1923)

You, Farmer, shame on you, why do you speak
of women with such rudeness and contempt?
No lady would consent to speak to you.
You should not move your muddy feet off your
own carpet. Farmer, go back to your spade!

What do you know of Shakespeare? How can you,
a Farmer, be the peer of such a guide?
Have not you heard of Manfaluti?[15] No?
Well, what you need to learn is more about
beetroots. Not yours the struggles of the brave!
Be prudent! Farmer, go back to your spade!
What do you know of God or of God's house?
What do you care for minstrels or the friend?
Bring out your sickle, rake and crooked hoe!
If you must speak, then speak of cows and seeds
and furrows! Farmer, go back to your spade!

Your talk should be of ewes and lambs and wool,
of milk and butter, and of curds and whey.
The things you care about are hay and leeks.
The *mollá*, bless him, was as stupid as
his donkey. Farmer, go back to your spade!

Your plane tree has borne fruit. Your ass is just
a braying donkey. The phenomenon
of love means nothing to a boor like you.
No lady would consent to speak to you.
Save your breath! Farmer, go back to your spade!

The things you love are straw and barley. Go
back to your farm and reap your harvest there!
Do not be fooled by your own brainless talk!
Start listening to the voice of reason. It
will tell you, Farmer, go back to your spade!

I do not know who bore you, but I'm sure
your mother was of better stock than you.
Remember every morning this refrain:
Shame and disgrace on that fictitious name!
No lady would consent to speak to you.

In verse and prose I have replied to you.
Never again rush into war with women!
Having been vanquished, cease to spurn us! This
is the advice which women send to you.
Accept it! Farmer, go back to your spade!

"A Poem by Homá Mahmudi"
(in the periodical Álam-e Nesván, 1922)

O Zephyr, carry to Iranian men,
descendants of Sásán[16] and of the Keys,[17]
a message from Homá: If you are men,
read this from start to finish! Gallant youths,
distinguished gentlemen, remember that
your women too are offspring of the Keys!
If there had been no women, then there would
have been no kings called Key, no crown, no throne.
If women are inferior to men,
then Jesus certainly would not have been
brought through a woman's care into this world.
If in those bygone days the men had roamed
alone, their seed would have been valueless.
A woman nurtured you, made you a man.
Her being was the source of your existence.
No matter whether you are brave and bold,
whether you conquer great expanses of
this earth and place the crown upon your head,
yet even so you are a woman's son.
The rightful course is that you should speak well
of her and praise her, everywhere you go.

"A Poem by Homá Mahmudi in Reply to Criticism by Mrs. Senowbar Atábekián" (in Álam-e Nesván, 1922)

Ignoble babbler, you let loose your tongue
to attack women, just as drunkards do.
You called their faces black and dead. Did not
this crazy drivel cause you any shame?
You said that jewels are just earthenware.
Of course a driveler cannot understand
the meaning of the words of poetry.

Are women similar to bits of stone?
Are *huris* just like demons in your view?
You said that women slumber in a state
of ignorance. Yes, I know this. The men
have wished and tried to keep us ignorant.
If you would listen, you would learn that in
this wide world women too have won success.
But you do not know the environment
in which those lucky women spend their lives.
There, schools and colleges disseminate
knowledge and art; but here, we only have
a rotten education. In the end,
what can the victim of injustice do
but bow her head and sorrowfully hope?
We stay in corners of unhappy homes.
Their homes are beds of roses. Abjectness
and anguish lie in store for us. For them,
respect and happiness always at hand.
This dire injustice has made women men.
Our life is troubled; these are troubled times.
Someday the Judge will in His mercy bring
justice for women at the hands of men.

BANISHED FOR THE CAUSE

The risks for women eager to gain and spread knowledge in those days are shown by the case of Mrs. Fakhr-e Áfáq Pársá. In the unfavorable social climate of the time, she had to obtain her education by secret as well as open means. She then devoted herself to teaching girls in a primary school at Tehran. There she became acquainted with the headmistress, a well-educated lady and, as it turned out, the mother of her future husband, Farrokhdin Pársá (d. 28 February 1972), who was then editor of a newspaper called *Ershád (Guidance)*. They were married in 1912. Her husband moved in 1921 to Mashhad, where she continued to serve the cause of education by teaching at the Forugh School. At the same time she managed to get a license to publish a magazine called *Jahán-e Zanán (Women's World)* and proceeded to put it on sale. The city of Mashhad, being built around the shrine of the martyred Emám Rezá, was very much under the influence of the

Shi'ite Moslem clergy; and as few of them then held enlightened views, the utmost prudence and caution were needed to safeguard the magazine against attacks by reactionaries. Consequently, it only dealt in a very simple style with matters relating to basic principles of better living, hygiene, health, and the place of women in family life.

When her husband moved back to Tehran, Fakhr-e Áfáq Khánom continued to publish the magazine; but after the issue of a few numbers the authorities in Tehran banned it. This was done at the instigation of certain persons who objected to any sort of manifestation of women's existence and had no desire to see the then existing order in any way shaken. At the same time Fakhr-e Áfáq was banished to Qom (the city built around the tomb of the Emám Rezá's sister Fáteme-ye Ma'sumeh). For two years this honorable lady remained in exile until finally, after repeated letters to the capital and approaches to the authorities, she was allowed to return to Tehran at the time of Rezá Sháh the Great's accession to the throne (1925). Thereafter, she cooperated in the production of the magazine *Álam-e Zanán (Women's Universe)*. Her work as a writer brought her into close and cordial contact with the Patriotic Women's League, whose various activities gained much from her cooperation.

Her daughter, Dr. Farrokhru Pársá, graduated as a doctor of medicine and became Iran's first woman cabinet minister, serving as minister of education from 1968 to 1974.

ONE WAY OF MAKING
THE WOMEN'S FEELINGS KNOWN

Not long after the formation of the Patriotic Women's League, the well-known lawyer and journalist Ebráhim Khwájeh Nuri published a *Letter to Young People* in which the diehards scented a whiff of feminism; they interpreted it as a denunciation of the veil. He was prosecuted and summoned to appear in court. On learning of this, the league decided that all its members would be present at the trial. Accordingly, a group of veiled women went and sat in the public gallery of the court where they quietly listened

After the First World War

to Mr. Khwájeh Nuri's pleas in his own defense, which formed an instructive lesson for them. This step conferred special importance on the trial as a political case involving women, and probably opened the door to women's attendance at trials and other publicly held official gatherings.

There were several philanthropic and stalwart ladies in the Khwájeh Nuri family who worked to improve the status of women and to win openings for their talents. Mrs. Effat ol-Moluk Khwájeh Nuri, an accomplished and well-known artist, was active in social service and art teaching for many years. Mrs. Nozhat Jahángir devoted herself to the reform of women's prisons and girls' orphanages, where the conditions at that time were appallingly bad, and in the course of her work met with troubles and unpleasantnesses which ought to be told someday.

Sometimes men attended meetings of the Patriotic Women's League, to encourage the members and advise them how to pursue their struggle and how to resist the reactionary forces. Among those who came were Ebráhim Khwájeh Nuri, Dabir-e A'zam, and the distinguished scholars (later university professors) Sa'id Nafisi and Dr. Rezázádeh Shafaq.

THE FIRST WOMEN'S INTERNATIONAL CONGRESS IN IRAN

In 1932, after three distinguished Arab ladies named Nur Hemáda (from Beirut), Hanina Khuri (from Egypt), and Seyyeda Fátema (from Iraq), had come to Tehran to organize a Congress of Women of the East, the Iranian government appointed the late Mr. Owrang to guide and help them in the unprecedented task of arranging the sessions of a women's conference. The Patriotic Women's League, which was then led by Mastureh Afshár, accepted responsibility for their reception and entertainment.

The congress set up a number of committees. Its discussions were centered on the ever-increasing advances won by European women and the continuing deprivations suffered by the women of the Arab countries and of Iran, and on the need for vigorous campaigning and positive action by enlightened women.

The ladies attending the sessions all wore *chádor*s and veils which wholly covered their faces. Some of them bluntly expressed their feelings and, in particular, their sorrow and dissatisfaction over the general ignorance and illiteracy of Oriental women; but in spite of the blamelessness of such feelings, a good many of them judged such eagerness for change to be premature for the superstition-ridden, male-dominated women of the Eastern part of the world, and showed reluctance to attend the sessions and hear these subjects discussed—no doubt for fear of subsequent trouble with their own menfolk.

Even so the congress was important. The reports of its proceedings in the press had some influence on public opinion and probably more influence on the minds of statesmen.

A CONSTRUCTIVE REBEL

An earlier venture into journalism had been made by a woman who will always be remembered for this bold step and for her life of devoted service, namely Sadiqeh Dowlatábádi. For much of the period under review in this chapter, she was abroad.

Born into a family of the Shi'ite Moslem clergy, Sadiqeh Khánom rebelled against the restrictions of the traditional domestic life and came forth as a champion of the women's movement. She was a person of strong character and unshakable will. Her great-grandfather on her mother's side, Mollá Ali Hakim Nuri, was an eminent *mojtahed*[18] who resided at Esfahán and gave classes which were attended by large numbers of theology students. His two daughters also wished to gain benefit from his lectures, and he allowed them to come and sit in the class behind a screen. Among the participants were two brothers who were highly respected as *seyyed*s (descendants of the Prophet Mohammad's son-in-law Ali and daughter Fátemeh). On the day when these two young theologians achieved the degree and rank of *mojtahed*, Mollá Ali made a speech to the students in which he said, "I have two daughters, ages twenty-one and twenty-three, and they are classmates of yours behind this screen. Will any one of you who would like to become related to me please shut his book?"

None of them shut their books. Finally, Mollá Ali, who had the two brothers above all in mind, repeated the question, and the brothers, each of whom had previously been restrained by shyness and modesty, or by knowledge of his own poverty, from expressing willingness to become his teacher's relative, now plucked up courage and shut their books. The *mollá* then told them that since the rules of Islamic Law required a prospective husband to see his prospective wife once before the marriage, they must go behind the screen and choose their brides. The two brothers then went and looked at the two unveiled sisters. The elder brother asked for the hand of the younger sister, and the younger brother for the hand of the elder sister; the marriage contracts were concluded forthwith. Sadiqeh Dowlatábádi's mother was the granddaughter of one of these couples, namely Mir Ali Áqá and his wife Beygom Sáheb. Her father, Hájj Mirzá Hádi Dowlatábádi, was a well-known religious scholar and clergyman at Esfahán; he had several daughters and sons, for each of whom he provided education at home with the aid of teachers. When Sadiqeh reached the age of sixteen, however, arrangements were made for her marriage to an elderly man. In those days the consent of a daughter was not considered essential. At the same time Sadiqeh's father gave her a leather briefcase which he told her to open after his death. It contained her marriage contract, and she afterward learned that there was a clause in it empowering the wife to initiate a divorce as attorney for her husband. Her father had inserted this provision for his daughter's use in the event of conjugal discord.

In 1917 Sadiqeh Dowlatábádi founded a girls' school called Maktabkháne-ye Shari'at at Esfahán, where hitherto no educational facilities for girls had been available apart from private tutoring; and in the following year she established the Esfahán Women's Association, which in 1920 issued a periodical called *Zabán-e Zanán (Women's Voice)*. It was the first to be published in Iran under editorship of a woman and in furtherance of the awakening of Iranian women. Its appearance aroused the hostility of the fanatics, who stoned and looted her office. She then moved to Tehran and continued *Zabán-e Zanán* there, but soon found it necessary to leave her homeland.

She went to France in 1922 and devoted herself to the study of educational principles and methods. At the same time she wrote articles for French newspapers on the subject of the Moslem Iranian woman's right of independent management of her own property, and on the general superiority of the legal status of Moslem women compared with that of European women at that time. These articles attracted interest and provoked controversies in the French newspapers. In 1927 she obtained admission as the representative of the women of Iran to an international women's conference in Paris and delivered a speech which made a deep impression.

She returned to Iran during the early part of Rezá Sháh the Great's reign, when Iranian women were still secluded, but she herself never put on the veil. She received an official appointment as an inspectress of girls' schools and in her spare time devoted herself to social work. In 1937 the Ministry of Education appointed her to the presidency of the Ladies' Center, which had been established in 1935 at the wish of Rezá Sháh (as described in the next chapter). Although the Ladies' Center had lost its original function after the prohibition of the veil, the Ministry of Education wished to preserve the name of this institution, which was transformed into an educational and craft-training center for adult women and for retarded girls from the primary and secondary schools. Sadiqeh Dowlatábádi carried out the reorganization of the center and stayed at the head of it until her death in August 1961. She lived on the premises and, despite illnesses, never relaxed from her work for the mental and moral uplift of Iranian women.

THE FIRST UNVEILED IRANIAN WOMAN TEACHER

In 1928, when the Iranian government decided to send a headmaster and teachers to give history and geography lessons in the Persian mother tongue to children of Iranians living in Caucasia, an enlightened and cultured lady on the Ministry of Education's staff, by name Shams ol-Moluk Khánom, volunteered for the post and was sent to Tiflis. There she spent three years teaching in a mixed school[19] and at no time wore the veil. It was then that she met her husband, the distinguished writer Ali Javáher-e Kalám (d. 1976), who was one of her fellow teachers. She also gave talks to Soviet cultural societies. Later they were transferred to Istanbul on a similar mission to teach Iranian children in Turkey. She was the first Iranian woman teacher to be sent abroad and the first to cast off the veil. She became a member of the executive committee of the Ladies' Center and in recent times has been an active member of the Women's League of Supporters of the Declaration of Human Rights. She is the authoress of an interesting book entitled *Famous Women in Islam and Iran* (Tehran 1959).

THE CLASH OF OLD AND NEW IDEAS

Before the historic date of 7 January 1936, when Rezá Sháh the Great ordered the unveiling of Iranian women, the Ministry of Education had at the Shah's request taken steps to prepare the ground. Among these was the appointment of inspectresses from the ministry, who were to visit the girls' schools and through counsels and explanatory talks gradually make the pupils ready for the impending change. Mrs. Shams ol-Moluk Javáher-e Kalám was one of these inspectresses, and her assignment was to visit girls' schools in the southern section of Tehran. While working for the ministry as a teacher of Iranian children abroad, she had naturally not worn the veil, and after her return to Tehran in 1933, she had often, though not always, walked through the streets with her face uncovered. After the establishment of the Ladies' Center in 1935, she cast off the veil for good. At that time walking unveiled was generally still dangerous in the southern parts of Tehran and the Qanátábád district. The prevalent fanaticism over veiling was forcefully expressed to Shams ol-Moluk Khánom by the headmistress of a girls' school (called Nosratiye-ye Pardegián, i.e., Nosratiyeh School for Veiled Girls) in that district when she was sent to inspect it.

Mrs. Javáher-e Kalám writes:

One day I went into this school to carry out my task of encouraging the pupils to give up veiling. Imagine my amazement when I caught sight of the headmistress sitting on a chair just behind the doorway curtain! (In those days thick curtains used to be hung in front of girls' school doorways to prevent strangers from peeping at the girls when the doors were opened.) She held a cane. On seeing her in this posture, I asked the reason. "I am sitting here," answered the headmistress, "to give a proper punishment, a good beating, to any girl who comes to school wearing colored stockings." Naturally, my task seemed almost impossible in such circumstances, but I had to do it. I said to the headmistress, "If you beat the girls' feet with a big stick like that, maybe you will cause them serious foot injuries." "Never mind if their feet are crippled!" answered the headmistress. "That will be better for them than going to hell!"

I then walked into the classrooms and in the course of my inspection gave talks to the girls about the advantages of unveiling. I told them the good news that the black masks over their faces would soon be taken off, that they would be freed from restrictions and be able to play a useful part in society. On hearing my words, the young girls clapped their hands spontaneously. At this, the headmistress rushed into the classroom, cane in hand, shouting, "What is this shindy you have set off in the school?" Then she told me indignantly, "I do not need an inspectress. If I want one in future, I will inform you. Please depart forthwith!" The girls watched these scenes in amazement. I myself remained standing where I was and answered gently, "With respect, madam, I have not come here of my own choice. The ministry's instructions are that the girls must gradually be made aware that they are going to be released from their vile black veils, in accordance with the wish of H.I.M. Rezá Sháh. Perhaps you have not yet heard about the opening of the Ladies' Center, to which royal ladies and many other distinguished women have come unveiled." My words fell on deaf ears, and the headmistress declared, "I'll summon the police right now and have you arrested. I'll tell them that a godless unveiled woman has come here and is trying to pervert the people's daughters." Knowing that the police would protect me in such a situation, I was not dismayed. "I have no objection," I replied. "Please call them! Meanwhile I shall stay here." Realizing how the matter stood, the headmistress tried another ploy. "There's a mosque nearby and I'm going straightaway to see the prayer leader there. I'll ask him to decide how you should be dealt with." Then, after hurriedly putting on her veil and cloak and baggy ankle-length trousers, she went out to lodge her complaint with the local *mollá*. Although I remained in the school for some time, I did not see or hear anything more of her or of him while I was there. Afterward I learned that the local *mollá* had told the headmistress not to make an undue fuss over such an instance of the "prevailing lawlessness," which he described as "the chaos preceding the end of the world."

Mrs. Javáher-e Kalám's courage forced a number of fanatical headmistresses to change course and give up futile resistance.

GIRLS' EDUCATION IN THE PROVINCES

The movement to free Iranian women was not confined to Tehran. One of its most vigorous champions was Shams ol-Hayá Mansuri, who became the first provincial chief inspectress of girls' schools. She was the daughter of a patriotic constitutionalist of the province of Fárs. Like most literate women in former times, she learned reading and writing from her father. She was only twelve when she was sent to her future husband's home to be married. At the age of fifteen she began to think of resuming her education.

In 1921, this intrepid lady, who was then living in Tehran, set out with her two small children in a diligence (a two-horse coach) to revisit her birthplace, Shiráz. The roughness and insecurity of the road did not deter her. As it happened, the diligence broke down, and she and the children were thrown onto the road. It took them eleven days to reach Esfahán and seventeen more to reach Shiráz and set foot in her father's house.

She found the atmosphere in Shiráz much more advanced than in Tehran and resumed her studies there privately.

In 1923 the Shiráz Education Department decided to convert the Qor'án schools into primary schools, i.e., to install desks and benches in the classrooms and draw up a syllabus and introduce order and method into the teaching.

The need for female staff became apparent. At that time, however, upper-class women in Shiráz, though educated, were not prepared to serve the Education Department. Shams ol-Hayá Khánom broke this custom. She mustered five other brave and devoted ladies who shared her views, namely Táj ol-Moluk Hekmat, Álam-Táj Námus, Eshrat ol-Moluk Záre', Tal'at ol-Shari'eh Emámi, and Hájjieh Námus, and together they entered the education service as volunteers. Shams ol-Hayá began work as chief inspectress and liaison officer, and the other five as inspectresses of primary schools. This also led to their formation of the first Women's Union of Fárs. These ladies strove ardently in the daytime to improve the state of the primary schools and in the evening to increase their own knowledge by taking lessons as a group with private teachers. Unfortunately, progress was slow because the schools were under constant attack by persons who disapproved of making girls literate. They pulled down school signboards, raided or wrecked school buildings, and threw stones and earth at the heads of the six inspectresses, who wore the veil but could still be recognized in the streets.

There was a group of women troublemakers who came out every day and stoned the children as they passed and tore up their books shouting, "Literate girls become lewd wantons. Women can't claim equality with men. They're weaker. Their place is in the home."

In 1929 Shams ol-Hayá Khánom moved to the Education Department at Esfahán, and later she served as headmistress of a state secondary school for girls in Tehran. Since her retirement, far from sitting idly by, she has remained active in public service as an honorary inspectress in the provincial government of Esfahán and as president of the local Family Disputes Conciliation Board under the Family Protection Law of 1967.[20]

Liberal-minded women in other Iranian provinces likewise performed valuable services and gave proof of their worth and their good sense. Many stories are in circulation about women's exploits in Iranian Ázarbáiján during the Russian domination of the province (1908-1917), e.g., about stratagems which they employed to trap Russian troops; but in the absence of firm evidence, this brief mention must suffice. At Mashhad, Mrs. Forugh had founded a girls' school of the same name at an early date. At Shiráz, Mrs. Soghrá Khalili founded the Ehtejábiyeh (Seclusion) School in 1925; it was afterward renamed Badr Girls' School.

AN UNSUCCESSFUL EXPERIMENT

Shams ol-Hayá Mansuri and her five colleagues at Shiráz disliked having to shroud themselves in black and decided to change the color of their *chádor*s. They reasoned that if the purpose of veiling was to cover a woman's face and figure, the color of the cloth did not matter. Each of them made herself a dark-colored, taffeta *chádor,* and one day they all put these on and went out together. They had scarcely walked any distance before such a terrific hubbub blew up that they had to run separately for refuge in nearby houses. They suffered injuries to their heads and hands and were obliged to give up their innovation. The experiment of changing the color of the *chádor* was also tried in Tehran, and there too the result was unexpected and unpleasant. The wife of one of the parliamentary deputies clad herself in a dark brown *chádor* and in this garb attempted to enter a Moharram ceremony (commemoration of the Emám Hoseyn's martyrdom)[21] which was being held in the parliament house for the benefit of the deputies. But no sooner had this woman with a slightly different-colored covering appeared than the other women at the gathering went for her. She was badly beaten up before the parliamentary ushers rescued her and took her aside.

The colored *chádor* did not, of course, differ from the black *chádor* in shape and cut; it similarly enveloped the whole body and had a veil which covered the face. The motive for the color change, on which certain reforming women were so insistent, was primarily to get rid of the gloomy funereal spectacle which used to be presented by women walking in the street, and which used to draw jibes such "black crow" or "ink bottle" from the men. Iranian ink bottles in those days had broad bottoms and narrow tops with white wadding (instead of corks) and did indeed look rather like women in black *chádor*s and white veils. A secondary motive was to relieve the excessive heat which gathered under the black cloth in summer sunshine; with colored materials it could be less irksome. The opponents of this move feared that the change of color would lead to a change of form and to a gradual breakdown of the fence which they had built for the purpose of confining women. The slightest sniff of fresh air, so they thought, would upset the women's obedience and subservience to the men.

THE THEATER IN THE CAUSE OF WOMEN'S UPLIFT

As earlier mentioned, attendance at public entertainments, theaters and cinemas used to be restricted to men and prohibited to women, veiled though they were.

The idea that the theater might be used to expose the deplorable position of women and help women to see the harm of their way of life occurred to the mind of Ahmad Mahmudi Kamál ol-Vezáreh.[22] At first in his own home, and afterward in the hall of the Zoroastrian community, he produced a number of plays in which his brother Mohsen and most of the ladies of the Mahmudi family appeared on the stage. Leading parts were taken, and truly well performed, by Kamál ol-Vezáreh's daughter Fátemeh Mahmudi, by his sisters Malek-Táj Mahmudi and Hamdam Mahmudi, and by Homá Mahmudi (whose services to the community have been related above.[23]

One notable performance by Kamál ol-Vezáreh's kinsfolk (for the most part kinswomen) was their acting of the still very popular play *Ja'far Khán az Ferang ámadeh (Ja'far Khán's Return from Europe)* by Hasan Moqaddam, which had first been produced—for men—by the Young Iran Association in 1922. It served well as a lesson for retarded women. Its theme is the homecoming of Ja'far Khán, the son of a superstitious, illiterate family, after some years of far-from-profound study in Europe. His behavior shows that he has learned nothing of the sciences and skills of those lands, but has only bothered about copying outward appearances. On his return he has to face his female relatives, all of them simpleminded and ignorant. Ja'far Khán's use of French words and absurd Persian translations of foreign phrases and his affected gestures and actions bewilder the other members of the family. At the same time, Ja'far Khán's mother and fiancée and other relatives reduce him to despair with their notions and superstitions. The play is equally forceful in its satire of ignorant, old-fashioned people and of the superficial young imitators who at that time were numerous. Its comic presentation of the relationship between a mother of the former type and a son of the latter type is an effective piece of social criticism.

Another play done by this liberal-minded and patriotic family was named *Mahrum ol-Vekáleh*.[24] They also acted some foreign plays which they had translated and adapted to the Iranian environment. Many years earlier, before the First World War, one of the Tehran bazaars (Bázár-e Kenár-e Khandaq) had been smitten by fire, and, of course, as there was no insurance in those days, the victims had lost everything. Kamál ol-Vezáreh had then organized a special women's theatrical show and distributed the proceeds, totaling five hundred *tomán*s, among those who had suffered loss in the disaster.

The high-minded Mahmudi family, who are remembered as pioneers and leaders of the constitutional movement, also deserve esteem for their contribution to the awakening of Iran's women.

ALI AKBAR SIÁSI'S PLAY MÁH-PÁR AND THE ACTRESS VARTO TARIÁN

Máh-Pár, a play in four acts by Dr. Ali Akbar Siási, gives a vivid impression of the evils and domestic and social effects of veiling, and won great popularity among enlightened people, especially women. A production of the play was staged in the Zoroastrian-owned Cyrus theater, with the gentlemen of the audience seated in the hall and the ladies in the capacious balcony. The play, which is in four acts, has a plot roughly as follows: A superficially Europeanized husband neglects and ill-treats his cultured and beautiful wife, who is named Máh-Pár. At the same time, he incessantly and quite unscrupulously concocts stratagems to seduce the cloistered women of other families, including those of his own friends. His wife fails in her efforts to regain his love and to deflect him from mischief. Finally, she concocts a stratagem herself. Taking advantage of the concealment afforded by the veil, she and her sister secretly station themselves on her husband's path. She starts flirting with him, and he praises her charming ways and witty talk with the most exaggerated compliments. Then, professing to be madly in love with her, he begs her favor. So it goes on until one day he asks her to come to the outer court of his house and takes her in. During all the time that her husband has been pressing his attentions, Máh-Pár has not unveiled her face. She has only promised to do so at a later date. As soon as they arrive, she starts walking toward the inner court, and he gets excited and stops her. Then he tells her that he has a vicious wife in the house who must not know about their secret. At this juncture Máh-Pár (whose part was played by Varto Tarián) lifts the veil from her face. With mingled anger and pride, she says some telling words to her husband: "You should be ashamed, man! I am your wife, the same woman who's not good enough for your affection when she's your dependent. But when I'm in another garb, you declare in my presence that you love me and will be faithful to me. What a vile thing it is that you flighty men should keep us women in the captivity of the veil, and keep Iran five centuries behind the caravan of civilization, just to make it easier for you to pursue your whims!" The play, with its impressive—and authentic—passages such as this, gave a warning to the men and women in the audience and prompted them to think about matters which had become too familiar to be perceptible.

The applause for this final scene was long and heartfelt. Varto Tarián relates that she became so enthusiastic as she uttered the words that she could not contain herself for joy. After the play was over, the women in the audience embraced her, and one of them said, "It's just what happened to me. How did you find out?" Another said "It would be such a help if you would speak to my husband for me and give him a proper scolding!"

Varto Tarián was the first woman who gave public recitations of Persian poetry. She recited *ghazal*s (sonnets) at the Barbad[25] Club and the Young Iran Association. Talented and artistic, and at the same time patriotic, she acted in several other plays, each of which sounded a specific note of social criticism. Unfortunately, as people never dared to bring cameras to these theatrical performances, we have no photographs of the scenes. Her husband was an army officer. On account of his wife's persistence in play-acting and deliberate use of her art as a means of helping women to see clearly and prepare for change in their way of life, he was several times subjected to interrogation and one occasion suspended for several months. Varto Tarián herself was forced to make some of her stage appearances under the assumed name Láleh.

By composing this play, Ali Akbar Siási stirred and delighted the contemporary generation of enlightened and discontented women. At the same time he gave errant and neglectful husbands a warning signal that such ways can lead to danger.

NOTES

1. See the translations in appendix B.
2. E.g., among the foreign girls' schools run by missionaries, the English Behesht-Áyin School and the French Rudábeh School at Esfahán, and the French Jeanne d'Arc School at Tehran, as well as the American school.
3. The American journalist Vincent Sheean, in his book *The New Persia* (New York 1927), has recorded the first governmental employment of a woman in such a capacity. She was Sárá Khánom, an Iranian widow whose Northern Ázarbáijáni husband had been killed by the Bolsheviks. After her return to Iran, she was unwilling to veil herself and to live in idleness and dependence; after much persistence, she finally got work with the government through the help of Mohammad Ali Foroughi (prime minister in 1925-26 and 1941-42 and a distinguished writer). In 1926 she was sent as one of Iran's representatives to an international exhibition at Philadelphia.
4. See note 1, chapter II, p. 22.
5. Endowments for religious or charitable purposes, such as the upkeep of mosques, schools, hospitals, and such. There are also "*private vaqfs*," i.e., endowments for the benefit of the testator's descendents.
6. *Dár ol-Mo'allemát.*
7. Translator's note: the authoress.
8. See pp. xvii-xviii.
9. See pp. 97-98.
10. See pp. 92 and 121.
11. *Daneshsará-ye Moqaddemáti-ye Dokhtarán.*

12. *Jam'iat-e Nesván-e Vatankhwáh.*
13. The great champion of Iran in the mythical part of Ferdowsi's *Sháhnámeh.*
14. The stonemason of the poet Nezámi's romance, who for love of Shirin toiled unremittingly but in the end in vain.
15. An Egyptian short-story writer whose works were very popular throughout the Middle East (1876-1924)
16. Reputed ancestor of the Sásánid dynasty (A.D. 229-652).
17. A mythical dynasty in Ferdowsi's *Sháhnámeh.*
18. See note 7, chapter III, p. 54.
19. The school was called Ettefáq-e Iránián.
20. See p. 122.
21. See note 1, chapter II, p. 22.
22. He was the son of Mahmud Khán Mahmudi Mosháver ol-Molk, also known as Káshef ol-Setáreh.
23. See p. 72.
24. The name, which means "unsuccessful parliamentary candidate," was humorously formed on the model of an Iranian title. (Titles were abolished in 1925.)
25. Minstrel of the court of King Khosrow Parviz (590-628) and reputed inventor of the Iranian system of music.

V

THE DAYBREAK

THE REFORMS OF REZÁ SHÁH THE GREAT

After the change of dynasty, Iran made great progress in many fields. Law and order prevailed everywhere. Plans to improve communication between the provinces were put into effect through the building of roads and of the Trans-Iranian Railway and through the introduction of aviation. The various branches of the civil service and the armed forces were modernized and enlarged. Modern professions and industries grew in importance, and many factories were established. The judicial system was reformed, and codes of commercial, penal and civil law were enacted. The Civil Code made some improvements in the position of women, e.g., by fixing the minimum age of marriage at fifteen for girls (eighteen for boys) and by recognizing the right of wives to work.

For the full success of these developments, it was necessary that the whole of the nation should be educated and thereby enabled to participate. In 1934, the Majles approved laws for the creation of a number of additional men's and women's teacher training colleges (to make good the shortage of teachers), and for the establishment of Tehran University (through incorporation of existing colleges and creation of new faculties).

Although real progress had been made in girls' education, this had been slow in relation to other advances and to the country's needs. Apart from a small minority, half of the nation was not yet ready to participate in the tasks which lay ahead.

It appears to have been in 1932 (the year of the Congress of Women of the East) that Rezá Sháh the Great came to the conclusion that the pace of women's advancement in Iran must be accelerated.

From about then onward, high-ranking wives and daughters sometimes appeared at official gatherings without veils, though it must be admitted that they were few and that the occasions were infrequent. The Ministry of Education began to encourage teachers who ventured out with uncovered faces, and later (as related in the previous chapter) to send inspectresses who gave lectures to delighted schoolgirls on the need for participation and on the evils of veiling.

THE FORMATION OF THE LADIES' CENTER

On 12 May 1935 the Women's Teacher Training College was the scene of an event which deserves remembrance as a significant advance for women.

The college's teachers and about twenty other women concerned with education received invitations to a reception in one of the rooms at the college's premises on Zahir ol-Eslám Street, adjoining Sháhábád Avenue. The contemporary minister of education, Ali Asghar Hekmat, and two high officials, Dr. Valiolláh Khán Nasr and Mr. Shamsávari, were to be present.

The minister brought tidings which gladdened the hearts of his hearers. H.I.M. Rezá Sháh, he told them, had orally commanded that their group of educationists should not limit their efforts to teaching, but should also set up a permanent organization to interest other ladies in pioneering social services and activities which would enable Iran's women to escape from seclusion and catch up with the rest of the world's women. In addition to the women teachers, two prominent statesmen's wives, Mrs. Mansureh Vosuq and Mrs. Pari Hosám, had been invited and were present at the reception.

No program of action was discussed on that day; indeed, veiling was not even mentioned. Mrs. Hájar Tarbiat was elected president of the new organization, and the members were asked to draw up articles of association for the minister's approval. Weekly meetings were arranged, and at the first meeting the name Ladies' Center[1] was adopted. The meetings continued to be held at the Women's Teacher Training College until premises on Sepáh

Avenue were rented. Weekly lectures were arranged, and the membership grew.

Following is a list of the ladies and gentlemen who spoke at the meetings in the first half-year of the center's existence. At the inaugural meeting, address by Mrs. Tarbiat, lectures by Mr. Esfandiári (speaker of the Majles) and Mrs. Tarbiat. At subsequent meetings, lectures by Mrs. Pari Hosám (girl guide leader), Mrs. Betul Homáyun Alamir, Mr. Loqmán Adham Hakim ol-Dowleh, Mrs. Ashraf Nabavi, Mr. Hájj Áqá Khán Tekini,[2] Miss Sadiqeh Dowlatábádi, Mr. Hasan Vosuq,[3] Miss Sháyesteh Sádeq, Miss Shams ol-Zohá Neshát. At the meeting on 20 March 1936 a debate was held with four students as the speakers, two of whom, Forugh Kiá and Tusi Háyeri, were girls, and two boys, Hoseyn Khatibi and Ezzatolláh Kheradmand. The question was, "Can women take part in the community's affairs? Are they capable of performing those social functions which have usually fallen to men?" The girls answered positively, the boys negatively, and the debate was very interesting and exciting.

At a subsequent meeting of the Ladies' Center, the royal decision permitting women to enter the university was made known, and a number of the members immediately declared their willingness to embark on higher studies.

Rezá Sháh the Great's choice of the women teachers to start the process of bringing women into civic life was deliberate. He conferred this honor on them in order that the basic aim might be properly explained and the way ahead clearly shown.

The articles of association of the Ladies' Center were as follows:

> The Ladies' Center of Iran is instituted under the honorary presidency of H.I.H. Princess Shams Pahlavi and the patronage and supervision of the Ministry of Education, for the purpose of achieving the undermentioned objectives:
> 1. To provide adult women with mental and moral education, and with instruction in housekeeping and child rearing on a scientific basis, by means of lectures, publications, adult classes, etc.
> 2. To promote physical training through appropriate sports in accordance with the principles of health preservation.

3. To create charitable institutions for the support of indigent mothers and children having no parent or guardian.

4. To encourage simplicity of life-style and use of Iran-made goods.

5. This center has legal personality in accordance with article 587 of the Commercial Code, and its president is the legal representative of the center.

Besides the president, Mrs. Hájar Tarbiat, the members of the center's executive committee were: Nosrat Taslimi, Badr ol-Moluk Bámdád, Batul Shiváyi, Ashraf Nabavi, Mehrbánu Sepáhi, Akhtar Kámbakhsh, Batul Homáyun Ehteshámi, Fakhr-e Irán Ghaffári, Afsar ol-Moluk Aryáyi, Táj ol-Moluk Hekmat, Fakhr-e Ozmá Arghun, Sháhbánu Fakhr, Monir Afkham Afkhami, Sadiqeh Riázi, Mehr-e Anvar Sami'i, Esmat ol-Moluk Dowlatdád, Shams ol-Moluk Javáher-e Kalám, Parvin E'tesámi, Pari Hosám, Qamar Kiá, Shams ol-Zohá Neshát.

The center soon began to function in the ways laid down in its rules and organized not only lectures, but also exhibitions, sports clubs and adult classes. Mrs. Tarbiat, who is one of Iran's most distinguished ladies,[4] was indefatigable in her leadership of these efforts for the good of the community.

One of the center's main purposes was to promote abandonment of the veil, and in this some progress was gradually achieved. The women who joined the center began to persuade their relatives one one by one to drop the black shroud, and the lectures emboldened other ladies to do likewise, so much so that at every lecture session or meeting held by the center more unveiled women could be seen at the back of the audience, behind the schoolmistresses who sat in front. It must be stressed that in those days, when violent and ignorant fanaticisms were still widespread, real courage was needed for a woman to step out of doors with her face showing. Admittedly, the police had received secret orders to protect unveiled women, but, out of the eye of the police, in empty streets passing women who wore no veil ran a strong risk of verbal abuse and physical attack with sticks or stones. Insulting the pioneers of women's freedom was no monopoly of men; fully equal to them in this respect were women of the lower classes

The Daybreak

indoctrinated with the notion that to lift the veil is a woman's worst sin and disgrace. Things reached such a pitch that some of the pioneer unveilers who lived in the southern part of Tehran reluctantly had to put on veils when they set out, then take them off and hide them in their handbags when they reached the upper part of the city, and then again put them on when they approached their homes.

Most of the gatherings of the Ladies' Center took place in the presence of H.I.H. Princess Shams Pahlavi and H.I.H. Princess Ashraf Pahlavi. The lecturers were by no means all women; some of them were men of eminence in public life.

A MOMENTOUS DECREE

Eight months after the formation of the Ladies' Center, it was learned that a big educational function was to be held on 7 January 1936[5] in the presence of H.I.M. Rezá Sháh. The scene of this great occasion was the (men's) Teacher Training College (now the Faculty of Education of Tehran University on Roosevelt Avenue). At the express command of the Sháhansháh, it had been decided that all the women teachers in the capital should attend without veils. They duly made their way to the college.

The authoress well remembers the looks of astonished disbelief on the faces of the men in the streets and the crowds lining the royal route when they saw some schoolmistresses walking by, unveiled.

These people were too confused to perceive that the centuries-old structure of outworn customs and notions was about to crumble. They did not realize that Iran's women, being no longer shut away from the light which knowledge and understanding bring, would henceforth be showing their faces and making heard their voices to the whole nation and not just to close relatives; that they would no longer depend solely on men, whether jealous and fanatical or attentive and kind, for their bread and water; that they would emerge from their cocoon and acquire personality.

On reaching the college, the schoolmistresses were shown to the places in its auditorium which had been allotted to them. Then, into this great hall, came the royal ladies, each a pioneer of women's freedom and each showing her face: H.I.M. the Empress and her daughters, Princess Shams and Princess Ashraf. Then, amid the applause of the assembled teachers, the wives of the ministers and generals entered and took their seats. Some of the elderly ladies among them, however, were visibly so upset by the loss of facial cover that they stood almost the whole time, looking at the wall and perspiring with embarrassment. Then, accompanied by the ministers and generals, came the king of the country, Rezá Sháh Pahlavi.

The Sháhansháh began his historic speech, which the women who were present still carry inscribed on their hearts, with the words "My mothers! My sisters!" and he ended by saying, "I prefer not be to assertive. I am not going to express joy over the action which has been taken. I have no desire to draw distinctions between the Iran of today and the Iran of other days. But, ladies, know that this is a great day, and use the opportunities which are now yours to help the country advance . . ."

After that day, women wearing veils were forbidden to circulate in the main streets of Tehran and the provincial cities. They were guided by the police into side streets. This action involved the Iranian government in not a few difficulties, e.g., at Mashhad where agitation led to violence. The women themselves at first found their new situation strange and startling. Thanks to the unshakable strength of will of the nation's liberator, the difficulties were overcome.

From then onward, civil servants in the provinces were compelled to bring their wives without veils to official celebrations and receptions given by governors and heads of departments. Often old friends and even kinsfolk then met each other's wives and daughters for the first time. These cold and awkward gatherings served toward the fulfillment of a vitally important national purpose.

It was a period of great prosperity for dressmakers and hairdressers. One sign of the times was the appearance of milliners' shops in the main streets of Tehran and the provincial cities.

THE TOP PUPILS OF THE YEAR 1935

In the course of the ceremonies on 7 January 1936, two schoolgirls were presented to the Rezá Sháh the Great and congratulated by him. They were Monir Asfiá, who had come out top of grade ten in the secondary schools of Tehran, and Hurásá Fasá (later Mrs. Shokuh) who had come out top of the first year in the secondary schools of the whole country in June 1935. Hurásá Fasá was a granddaughter of Yusof Rishár (Richard), the founder of the Women's Teacher Training College and of ten girls' schools and the first head of the Department of Public Instruction for Women.

When the ceremonies ended, the teachers and other guests walked out of the hall into the college garden to line the path of the royal procession. The Sháhansháh, who was cheerful and smiling, then stopped and spoke very kindly to Monir Asfiá. In order to give this girl a lasting token of his esteem, he ordered that she should be photographed with him. One of the photographers hastened forward and photographed them, but, unfortunately, it afterward transpired that he had run out of plates and had been too embarrassed to say so.

Mrs. Hurásá Shokuh was not only one of the first two schoolgirls presented to a Sháhansháh of Iran. Later she was to be one of the first two ladies summoned to a royal salaam. This was on 26 October 1957, when she received the Crown Medal (Fifth Class) for her services to the Ministry of Health. The other lady then summoned was Mrs. Effat Sami'ián. In 1974 Mrs. Shokuh was again honored, by the award of the Imperial Medal (Fifth Class).

WOMEN GAIN ACCESS TO HIGHER EDUCATION

A few months later came another memorable day, when the minister of education conveyed to the Ladies' Center the glad tidings of a further royal action. H.I.M. Rezá Sháh had decided that women holding the necessary qualifications would be allowed to enter all university faculties and to pursue the courses of study together with men. Moreover, special arrangements would be made to enable schoolmistresses to attend the lectures at the required hours.

Problems arising from the shorter duration of girls' (relatively to boys') secondary schooling at that time were overcome by special arrangements (which have already been described[6]).

This was a wonderful gift for women eager to acquire knowledge and for families willing to let their daughters go in for higher education. It was quite a while, however, before people generally dared to send girls into an environment where they would freely mix with boys. Everybody waited for somebody else to take the first step, with the idea of letting others bear the blame in the event of a mishap.

Consequently, the first group of girls to enter Tehran University in September 1936 numbered only twelve. Some went into the Higher Teacher Training College (faculty of education), others into the faculties of sciences and arts. All are scholarly and industrious women, and each has made a name for herself in public or social service.

Their names are: Dr. Shams ol-Moluk Mosáheb (now a senator); Dr. Mehrangiz Menuchehrián (lawyer, now a senator); Zahrá Eskandari (secondary-school teacher); Batul Sami'i (secondary-school teacher); Tusi Háyeri (secondary-school teacher); Sháyesteh Sádeq (scholar of Persian and French literature); Táj ol-Moluk Nakha'i (secondary-school teacher and inspectress); Dr. Forugh Kiá (doctor of medicine); Dr. Zahrá Kiá (Khánlari) (university professor); Badr ol-Moluk Bámdád (now an adviser to the Ministry of Education); Seráj ol-Nesá (from India); and Sháhzádeh Kávusi (had to withdraw from the University).

The handful of girl students did not find life easy in the unfamiliar surroundings of their respective faculties. They usually stayed together in a corner to avoid glances. The boys mostly seemed ill at ease in the new situation. While the girls had deliberately and prudently prepared themselves for entry, the boys were completely disconcerted. For most of them, mixing with girls was something quite unforeseen. They therefore avoided talking to the girls or even answering them, and if there was no escape they blushed from ear to ear and stuttered. At the lectures, wherever a girl sat, the bench on each side of her stayed empty.

Certain elderly professors were just as nervous as the boy students about speaking to the girls and looking them in the face. One girl, then in her second year at the university, asked a professor who had shut his eyes when replying to a question from her, "Don't you trust your eyes, professor?" He was puzzled and asked, "What do you mean?" "I mean why won't you look at girls?"

As for the librarian, the sight of the girls side by side with the boys distressed him so much that he marked off a special corner like a harem where the girls might safely sit. This brought a rebuke from Dr. Isá Sadiq, then dean of the three faculties of education, science, and arts, who informed him, "If you think that the government has forced girls to come here because it has neglected to open a special college for them, you are mistaken. They have been admitted in order that boys and girls may learn the civilities of mixing and living together and acquire the habit of cooperating in activities for the good of the community. In this manner they will clear away the notions and customs which bisect the fabric of Iranian society."

Notwithstanding adverse social factors, and intrigue and sabotage which would need lengthy telling, this expert educationist (Dr. Isá Sadiq) was soon able to create a more favorable atmosphere, with the result that families began to send their daughters as students and to disregard the insinuations of ill-wishers.

It will be enough to describe just one of the malicious plots which were concocted with obvious intent to discredit Dr. Sadiq's policy of encouraging cooperation of boys and girls in service to the community. Two or three years after the admission of girls to the university, some boy and girl students clubbed together in the days before Nowruz (the Iranian New Year on 21 March) and worked long and hard to organize a convivial celebration with the traditional bonfire on Chahárshanbe-ye Suri (the Wednesday before Nowruz). (The bonfire symbolizes the end of dark days and the burning away of past evils.) It was arranged that the bonfire should be lit in a certain large courtyard, and that the girl students, whose number had now risen, should form a ring round the fire and the boys should stand behind them and all should sing a Nowruz song.

Probably at the suggestion of an agitator outside the university, some boy students acting in concert stationed themselves just behind the girls and joined hands and all at once pushed, with the intention of driving the girls so close to the fire that they would get scorched or burned. This odious design was spotted by other students just as it was being put into operation and was stopped in time; but the uproar and commotion took all the expected fun and joy out of the party.

THE FIRST WOMAN UNIVERSITY LECTURER

In the remaining five years of Rezá Sháh the Great's reign, women began to find opportunities of governmental and professional employment as well as work in the expanded teaching profession. They took part in athletics and sports and joined the Flying Club and learned to pilot airplanes. Many poorer women found work in the new textile mills. This was a time when gathering storm clouds of world war began to cast threatening shadows over the future.

The Ladies' Center, whose original purpose had been fulfilled by the unveiling, remained in existence and worked for the cause of adult women's uplift under the devoted leadership of Sadiqeh Dowlatábádi (1937-1961).[7]

It will be fitting to end this chapter with a few words about the first two women university teachers; about one of the first women university students, who became a lawyer and has done much for the cause of women's legal rights; and about a great poetess who rebuked discrimination and social injustice in unforgettable verses written at that time.

The first woman to become a university lecturer was Mrs. Amineh Pákraván. She was a granddaughter of Mohammad Khán, the nephew and brother-in-law of Shaykh Mohammad Khán Moshir ol-Dowleh.[8] He had gone to Europe in his youth for further study and had married the daughter of an artist who was employed in the Sèvres porcelain factory. He and his French wife had a son, Hasan Khán, who afterward went to Turkey to stay with Moshir ol-Dowleh (then ambassador at Istanbul) and while there married the daughter of the Austrian consul. They had two daughters, named Amineh and Fátemeh. Amineh was born on 18 November 1890. After their father's death in Paris, the two girls were brought up by their mother in Europe until her death left them entirely on their own. Their cousin on the father's side, Shaykh Mohammad Khán Sadiq-e Hazrat, then took steps which led to a decision by Mozaffar ol-Din Sháh that their travel expenses should be paid and that they should be sent to Iran. The nature of the journey at that time, and the unfamiliarity of the girls with their fatherland's ways, presented all sorts of problems for them, especially after Tiflis when they were required to put on veils for their homecoming and to behave like veiled women. Not long afterward Amineh married Mr. Fathollá Pákraván, and Fátemeh married Mr. Farzáneh. Amineh had two children, a daughter and a son. Her marriage proved impermanent and ended in divorce, and her daughter died. Her son, Hasan Pákraván, rose to be a general in the army and afterward (in the late 1960s) served Iran as ambassador to France.

Amineh Khánom was a learned woman with a great capacity for scholarship and research and at the same time a very modest person. She was appointed to the staff of Tehran University as lecturer in the history of art in 1934, two years before the admission of female students to the university. Strangely enough, it was not thought wrong for a woman to teach male students.

Amineh knew French, German and English thoroughly, as well as Persian. She wrote a number of historical novels in French,[9] which vividly and accurately depict real events. One of her books, a biography of Áqá Mohammad Khán (the founder of the Qájár regime), was translated and published in 1953 by the French Institute in Iran. In France, the Rivarol prize was awarded to her.

Various other works (historical essays and such) which Amineh Pákraván wrote were still unprinted when she passed away on 14 July 1958.

THE FIRST WOMAN PROFESSOR

Eight years after the appointment of Amineh Pákraván to a lectureship, a woman, Dr. Fátemeh Sayyáh, was appointed to a professorship at Tehran University.

Dr. Fatemeh Sayyáh, whose father's name was Aqá Ja'far Rezázádeh Sayyáh, was born in the Soviet Union and did her studies, which culminated in her doctorate, in that country. She came to Iran in 1942 and contributed effectively to the women's struggles. In the previous four years she had been employed as a lecturer in the arts faculties of various Soviet universities. She became Iran's first woman university professor when the chairs of Russian language and literature and of comparative literature at Tehran University were awarded to her. For the millenary celebrations of Ferdowsi's birth organized by the Anjoman-e Ásár-e Melli (National Heritage Society), she wrote a long and profound essay which was published in French as well as Persian, and at the Congress of Iranian Writers held at Tehran in 1946 she gave a very interesting lecture. Later she was attached by the Ministry of Foreign Affairs to the Iranian delegation to the United Nations. She joined several of the women's organizations and went on various missions abroad as the representative of the Council of Women. Her cogent books and articles have been published in Persian and French. This scholarly lady has won honor for Iranian learning and, at the same time, has striven to enlighten the minds of Iranian women and guide the activities of the women's organizations.

THE FIRST WOMAN LAWYER

One of the entrants to the university in 1936 was Mehrangiz Menuchehrián, who took courses in philosophy, educational sciences and law. After her graduation, she devoted several years to legal studies and research in Iran, the United States, and Europe; and in 1947 Tehran University awarded the doctorate of law to her in recognition of a valuable thesis on delinquency and penal law. She then became the first woman in the Iranian legal profession. She practiced as an advocate from 1947 to 1968 and also served as professor of penal law at Tehran University from 1964 to 1968. She was one of the first two women senators, the other being Mrs. Shams ol-Moluk Mosáheb; they were appointed to the senate in 1963.

In her work and her writings, Dr. Mehrangiz Menuchehrián has always had special concern for the legal rights of women and children. She played an important part in the passage of the Family Protection Law of 1967.[10] She has also been active in charitable work, for the Red Lion and Sun Society[11] and as legal adviser to the National Association for the Protection of Children. As a member of the International Association of Women Lawyers, she has won esteem in legal circles abroad. It was an honor for Iran when she was elected president of this association and commended by the United Nations in 1968 for her work in the field of human rights. Her books on Iranian constitutional, civil, and criminal law are widely used and particularly valuable for their treatment of the status of women in these fields. She has also written a book on education and another on aesthetics.

A GREAT POETESS

It was during these years that Parvin E'tesámi, who is generally considered to be Iran's greatest poetess, produced her work.

The beautiful words of Parvin's poetry are like seeds which grow and bear fruit in the field of every reader's heart. They make an impression which deepens and becomes indelible. Although literary appreciation and criticism are outside the scope of this book, it must be said that Parvin's poems have inspired many Iranians with a sense of duty and a determination to grapple with social problems by opening their drowsy eyes and arousing their latent strengths. She was one of the founding members of the Ladies' Center. Her presence was a source of pride to all the members, though it must be admitted that she often seemed unhappy with the environment and the problems. Her sensitive soul could be disturbed by slight things and lacked endurance. A minor annoyance caused her to burst into tears one day, after which she left the Ladies' Center and never returned.

This most honored of Iranian women was born at Tabriz in 1906. Her father, E'tesám ol-Molk, ranked among the foremost literary men of his time. After studying Persian and Arabic with her father, she entered the American Girls' School at Tehran and completed the course in 1924. She married her first cousin on her father's side in 1934, but they were incompatible and finally parted. From her childhood onward she devoted herself to poetry and wrote poems which had the quality of bright stars, spreading light in her country's darkness. She suffered from poor health and died in 1941. During her short life she uttered words which as long as the Persian language lives will not be erased from time's pages. Some of her best poems movingly describe the evils of poverty and social injustice and discrimination. Perhaps the most moving of them all is *"Zan dar Irán"* ("Women in Irán"), which expresses her thoughts about the lifting of the veil on 7 January 1936. A far-from-adequate translation of it will be found in appendix A.

NOTES

1. Kánun-e Bánuván.
2. Father of the authoress.
3. Prime minister, 1918-1919, with the title Vosuq ol-Dowleh.
4. See pp. 60 and 121.
5. 7 Dey 1314 in the Iranian calendar.
6. See p. 60.
7. See p. 78.
8. A diplomatist and moderate constitutional politician who held many cabinet posts and was prime minister for short periods in 1915, 1920 and 1924.
9. *Le prince sans histoire, Quatrième Génération,* and *Destinée Persane.*
10. See p. 122.
11. The Iranian Red Cross.

VI

TROUBLED TIMES

EFFECTS OF THE SECOND WORLD WAR

In the Second World War, Iran was again neutral, but after the German attack on Russia, the Soviet and British governments needed Iranian roads and railways and airspace as a "bridge to victory," and on 25 August 1941 they attacked Iran. On 16 September 1941 Rezá Sháh the Great was obliged to abdicate and depart from his beloved country. Large parts of the national territory remained under foreign occupation until 1946.

The wartime and postwar events had disruptive effects which were to hold back the nation's progress a long time.

AN UPSURGE OF REACTION

The reforms and developments of Rezá Sháh the Great's reign had matched the aspirations of patriotic, freedom-seeking Iranians and given promise of a bright future for the whole nation, including the female half of it. Girls and young women were now eagerly seeking knowledge in primary and secondary schools and in the faculties of Tehran University. Employment in the civil service and professions was gradually being opened to them. They had begun to obtain a better economic status. Previously, they had been totally dependent on men for their sustenance. When a wife happened to lose the husband for whom she lived and from whom she received her livelihood, there had normally been no way in which she could save herself and her children from the abyss of destitution except to endure the indignity and pain of dependence on close or distant relatives—or to clutch the lifeline of prostitution if she was young enough. No wonder women liked to see themselves as still young and blooming!

After September 1941, when the women's movement unexpectedly lost the support of the great royal patron who had done so much for their freedom and happiness, reactionary elements on every side seized the opportunity to start agitating and causing trouble. They strove with all the means at their disposal to undo the achievements of the previous period. In some of the provincial cities they managed quite easily to drive the women back into the prison of the veil, and even to get girls' schools closed on various pretexts. They knew that by belittling the mothers and paralyzing half the people they would weaken the fabric of society and thus promote their own treasonable aims. In the absence of Rezá Sháh's strong hand, these wreckers were not suppressed and punished. While that hand had been present, however, Iranian women had tasted freedom. They had studied at the university, started to earn honorable livings, and won positions of dignity. They would not passively surrender the bastions which they had captured to such foes.

THE WOMEN'S RESPONSE

In the face of these dangers, the enlightened women of Iran got together and formed two or three groups. One was the Women's (political) Party,[1] founded by Mrs. Safiyeh Firuz and later renamed the Council of Women.[2] Another was the Women's League, which in 1956 became the Women's League of Supporters of the Declaration of Human Rights. In 1944-1945 the Women's League published its own newspaper, *Zan-e Emruz (Women Today)*. Its members also wrote glowing articles for publication in other newspapers friendly to the cause, such as *Irán-e Má,* and even interviewed leaders of the reaction in the hope of silencing them by refutation of their arguments or explanation of the likely consequences of their dreadful designs. In fact, the adversaries were too stubborn to bend like willows before such gales; they knew what they were doing and how to act at the right moment.

Troubled Times

At the same time, the women's associations contacted patriotic politicians and sought help from the government. Although their approaches did not yield the hoped-for results, their courage in openly maintaining their stand had some effect in preventing a setback in the condition of the great mass of women in old-fashioned families, and in encouraging such women to resist oppression.

THE FIRST FEDERATIVE BODY

The women's associations saw the need to join forces in a combined stand against their opponents and in 1943 agreed to federate under a coordinating committee. Afterward a number of other groups adhered.

In 1956 a manifesto was published by the federative body, which consisted of the Council of Women of Iran, the Women's League of Supporters of the Declaration of Human Rights, the Women's Relief Committee of Tehran, the New Path Society, the Women Teachers' Association, and the Women Medical Practitioners' Center. An excerpt from the manifesto reads:

> Social developments in the last half-century have greatly changed our institutions and have faced women with heavy tasks and responsibilities. Obviously, the assumption of new duties warrants the grant of new rights. The enlightened and advanced women of present-day Iran cannot acknowledge social segregation. They insistently demand the rights which are their due.

There were, of course, times when the women's speeches and writings had consequences. Some liberal-minded newspapers, including *Zan-e Ruz*[3] in 1945, were banned. Martial law was then in force, and the authorities, under pressure from the agitators, imposed restrictions on the women's leaders and took recognizances from them. Far from quitting the fray, the women's associations persevered all the more resolutely in their work; for they knew that time does not go into reverse and that the nation's progressive forces were supporting them. The longer this state of affairs continued, the more the number of women's groups and the number of women joining them grew. As the years advanced, the prospect gradually brightened. The dark clouds began to disperse, and the sun of better fortune rose over the Iranian horizon.

THE FOUNDER OF THE COUNCIL OF WOMEN

At a time when few of the country's well-to-do women gave any thought to their national duties, one highly intelligent lady set herself the lofty aim of a life of unremitting devotion to social service. She was Mrs. Safiyeh Firuz, daughter of the late Hájj Mohammad Hasan Namázi, an Iranian merchant of Hong Kong.[4]

Safiyeh Khánom was born in Hong Kong in 1908. She can speak several foreign languages—English, French and Chinese—and has traveled widely in Europe, Asia and Africa. During the Second World War, when famine befell Iran in 1942, she started a women's clinic and personally served in it. Her husband was an army officer, and already in 1941, with the help of some other officers' wives, she had set up the Officers' Wives' Association for Aid to Soldiers' Families. She was a member of the Relief Committee in Tehran, and one of the first women to join the Red Lion Sun and other such bodies, to which she gave moral and material help unsparingly. As early as 1922 she had attempted to organize Girl Guides in Iran.

When the Iranian Women's movement fell into stagnation during the Second World War, Safiyeh Khánom took the initiative in organizing the Women's Party, later renamed the Council of Women of Iran, to combat the maneuvers of enemies of the women's renaissance. The council worked in conjunction with two other bodies which had been set up for the same purpose, namely the Women's League and the New Path Society. As the representative of the federated organizations, she attended various international conferences and gatherings of women, whom she acquainted with the hitherto scarcely known name of Iran. She represented her country at the International Women's Assembly at New York in 1946 and the Asian Women's Congress at Delhi in 1947, and attended the sessions of the Women's Rights Commission at Beirut in 1949 and Geneva in 1953, at which she was elected president and vice-president respectively.

Most of her time, however, she has spent in visiting and inspecting children's reformatories and women's prisons, and in rescue work for fallen women. She instituted classes where these women receive basic and vocational education and training in useful skills, and in this way she has saved a considerable number from the sink of corruption and misfortune. She was a founder-member of the High Council of Iranian Women. She has always taken a prominent part in the campaigns and actions which have been set afoot to press women's demands. She has also organized theatrical shows for the purpose of encouraging women with dramatic talent. In every social service that she has undertaken, she has shown the same tireless energy. The presidency of the Council of Women is still in the capable hands of Mrs. Safiyeh Firuz.

THE FOUNDER OF THE NEW PATH SOCIETY

Another lady who has greatly helped Iranian women to organize themselves, and to understand their legal rights and assume their responsibilities, is Mehrangiz Dowlatsháhi. After completing her university studies in Germany, she embarked on social work in 1946 on behalf of the Imperial Social Services Organization and the Prisoners' Aid Society. A subsequent post with the Development Institute has given her a close knowledge of the lifestyle of Iranian villagers. In 1955 she founded the New Path Society,[5] whose most important contribution has been the drafting of the Family Protection Law of 1967. The society has set up a welfare center in the southern part of Tehran for the purposes of raising the standard of living and level of knowledge among women, and providing classes to combat illiteracy and teach domestic science and child care. An international exhibition of women's activities with representation from thirty-two Asian and European countries, which it arranged, was most interesting and instructive. The New Path Society has always cooperated with the other women's organizations and taken part in their campaigns.

Mehrangiz Khánom, who is a very vigorous person, has made numerous journeys abroad, in the role of proxy for H.I.H. Princess Ashraf, to represent the High Council of Iranian Women at meetings of the International Council of Women. She has been cooperating since 1956 with the women's organizations of a number of countries and with international bodies such as the Commission on the Status of Women, the International Labor Conference, various seminars and such, and she has learned much from her experiences. Since the establishment of the High Council of Women, she has held important positions in it, including the vice-presidency, and has made impressive contributions to its work. She was a founder-member of the New Iran (Irán-e Novin) party in 1963 and became a member of the executive committee of its central council. It was she who brought into being the party's Kermánsháh branch. In 1976 Mrs. Mehrangiz Dowlatsháhi became the first woman head of an Iranian diplomatic mission when she was appointed ambassador to Denmark.

A LIFE GIVEN TO SOCIAL SERVICE

Another lady who contributed much to the women's movement in this uneasy period was Esmat ol-Moluk Dowlatdád.

Since higher education in Iran was not obtainable when Esmat ol-Moluk was young, she went to Europe in 1918 and studied at the Free University of Brussels. After graduation, she returned to Iran and resolved to give her life to social service. She first took a teaching post at the Women's Teacher Training College. Before long, the first state kindergarten in Iran, named the Shokufeh Kindergarten, was opened, and Esmat ol-Moluk Khánom was appointed headmistress. She ran it on the latest modern lines. Soon she was appointed head of the kindergarten department of the Ministry of Education, and while in this post she rendered very valuable services through her work to reform the training of kindergarten teachers. In 1935, when the Ladies' Center was set up, she became a member of its executive committee.

In later years she served on the executive boards of the Tehran Relief Committee and the Council of Women. She is a founding member of the High Council of Women's Association, which later became the Iranian Women's Organization. For a while she was president of the League of Women Supporters of the Declaration of Human Rights, and she is one of its most active members. By giving lectures and writing articles, she has striven to guide the minds of Iranian women and achieve full implementation of the Universal Declaration of Human Rights.

AN EXPONENT OF WOMEN'S RIGHTS IN ISLAM

While adversaries of women's advancement all too often invoke religion in support of their attitudes, scholars who have made profound studies of the subject are convinced that the laws of Islam, if properly understood and enforced, provide the best assurance of the good life and guarantee of women's legitimate rights. One such scholar is an Iranian woman, Dr. Qodsiyeh Hejázi.

This lady's father, Hájj Seyyed Mostafá Musavi Hejázi, is a learned Moslem clergyman of Tehran, and she herself is very devout and self-denying. Her mother is the daughter of another learned Moslem clergyman, Hájj Seyyed Musá Khalili.

While enjoying ample opportunity to study literary subjects and Arabic, Qodsiyeh Khánom had to face many difficulties, mainly arising from her family's disapproval, when she saw the need to study modern subjects also; but her remarkable zeal and assiduity enabled her to overcome every obstacle. She entered Tehran University and was graduated in 1952. Later she went to the University of Paris to do research and wrote a thesis on women's status which earned her the degree of doctor of law in 1961.

Among Dr. Qodsiyeh Hejázi's published works are one on women's crimes and one on marriage in the true faith of Islam. Her mastery of Arabic and French gives weight and substance to her writings, which show what a high position women hold in the teachings of Islam. Both in that respect and more generally, persons who do not know or understand the precepts of this illuminative religion will benefit from reading her books.

THE HIGH COUNCIL OF IRANIAN WOMEN'S ASSOCIATIONS

The Iranian women's movement owes much to the support of H.I.H. Princess Ashraf Pahlavi, who has always devoted time to social guidance with a view to fulfillment of the lofty aims of her brother, H.I.M. Mohammad Rezá Sháh Pahlavi. She has given particular attention to mothercraft training and to winning equality of women's rights with men's.

Having thoroughly acquainted herself with the work of the women's associations, H.I.H. Princess Ashraf consented to become their honorary president. This good news gave welcome testimony of the Sháhansháh's concern for the position of Iranian women and brought pride and joy to the hearts of the members. After a series of meetings in the princess's residence at Sa'dábád, they appointed a fifty-strong organizing committee and drew up articles of association for a new federal body called the High Council of Iranian Women's Associations. Seventeen groups of various kinds adhered when it came into being in 1959. In this way they combined their resources and activities for women's advancement in a modern-style organization under the patronage and guidance of a royal honorary president.

In the following years, the scale of activity grew so much that a new and expanded organization was founded on 20 August 1966 by H.I.H. Princess Ashraf, who throughout these years had carried on the guidance of the women's movement. The new organization, called the Women's Organization of Iran, took the place of the High Council of Women's Associations.

NOTES

1. *Hezb-e Zanán.*
2. *Showrá-ye Zanán.*
3. Translator's note: the authoress held its publication license and was its editor
4. He gave the Namázi Hospital and the modern piped-water supply system to his native city, Shiráz.
5. Jami'at-e Ráh-e Now

VII

THE WINNING OF EQUAL RIGHTS

THE WHITE REVOLUTION

After the withdrawal of the foreign troops in May 1946 and the liberation of Iranian Ázarbáiján in December of that year, there had been grounds for optimism about Iran's prospects in the reign of H.I.M. Mohammad Rezá Sháh Pahlavi, whose resolute patriotism was already evident and whose concern for social reform was soon made clear. On the other hand, harmful effects of the war persisted and grave problems had to be faced and solved. Before long, the dispute concerning the national rights in the southern Iranian oil industry opened the door to further tension and disturbance. After the finding of a solution to this problem in 1954, prosperity reappeared and constructive work was resumed; but Iran's advance was impeded by social injustices, of which the gravest were the status of the peasantry, who then formed more than two-thirds of the nation, and the status of the women, who formed one-half.

Naturally, women who had tasted education, and in particular those who had been able to become university graduates, were all strongly in favor of freedom and human dignity and equal rights for women. At the same time, many men, sometimes as a result of travel abroad, had discerned that there is a direct link between a nation's well-being and the abilities of its women. Above all, they had perceived the beneficial effect of women's working on the economic position of families. They had, therefore, come to the conclusion that women should be educated and treated as adults and allowed to engage in activities of value to the community. In opposition stood the forces of reaction and sabotage, who for years had exploited and profited from the weakness and ignorance of the masses. They had not changed their ideas, and they now saw themselves as guardians of the old order. When circumstances allowed, they had recourse to agitation and rabble-rousing; otherwise they bided their time.

Although the need for revolutionary reforms was obvious to all discerning Iranians, the dissensions and agitations which arose were such that H.I.M. the Sháhansháh finally decided that he must give a lead. The White Revolution of Shah and People was mapped out and then was announced by H.I.M. the Sháhansháh at a peasants' congress in Tehran on 10 January 1963. Among its original six points were land reform, electoral reform, establishment of a Literacy Corps, and profit sharing for workers. The six-point program was to be submitted to the people for their verdict in a referendum.

Soon afterward, the date of the referendum was fixed for 26 January 1963,[1] and the right to vote in it was defined in accordance with the existing electoral laws; i.e., the right to vote would be reserved to men and denied to the other half of the nation.

The women's associations of Iran were already indignant because women were being deprived of civic rights in municipal affairs. They were deeply angered when they learned that in this all-important referendum the old notion that only men inherit human rights would still prevail.

WOMEN AND MUNICIPAL COUNCILS

In May 1962, a doctor's wife, Mrs. Hakami, had been debarred from standing in an election for the Esfahán City Council, even though the municipal election law as it stood at the time was unqualified (as is the Persian language) by any distinctions of gender. Later in the same year, Mr. Asadolláh Alam's government drafted a law which expressly allowed women, to their great joy, to vote and be candidates in municipal elections. Unfortunately, owing to the still strong influence of reactionary elements opposed to women's progress, the government felt obliged to postpone the implementation of the new law. The women's associations considered this inequity to be no longer tolerable and prepared for a vigorous campaign against it. They made their feelings known by publishing articles and declarations of protest.

Normally, the Iranian women's associations hold an annual celebration on 7 January to commemorate the day of the unveiling in 1936, after first laying wreaths on Rezá Sháh's tomb in the morning. On the anniversary on 7 January 1963, however, they were in no mood to celebrate, and they published the following notice of cancellation: "In view of the continuing denial of legitimate rights to women, and in particular the government's failure to hold the local elections in which the right to vote has been given to women, the Women's Associations of Iran advise the male and female public that as a sign of protest the usual joyous celebration on 7 January will not now be held."

On the morning of the day, the women assembled in the mausoleum of Rezá Sháh at Shahr-e Rey and thence made their way to the prime minister's office, where their representatives met the prime minister and presented their demands to him.

WOMEN AND THE REFERENDUM

On learning about the electoral regulations for the referendum, the women's associations arranged a special meeting. After some heated discussion, they decided to express their welcome for the lofty reforming aims enunciated by the pilot of the nation, and to demand the right for Iranian women to vote on them in the referendum. This announcement led to appreciative demonstrations in all parts of the country, even in remote villages. Next they called a one-day strike for 24 January 1963; on that day women teachers in the primary and secondary schools, and women employed in the civil service and private institutions, concertedly withheld their labor. They made this gesture to show that the majority of the country's women were not immature but were able and determined to prove their competence in matters of concern to the community.

These moves by the women's associations forced the authorities to take action, despite the shortness of the remaining time and the uncertainty of the legal position, and notwithstanding the loudness of the hostile clamors. Every polling place was equipped with a special box into which women might cast ballots, even though these would have no legal worth. In this way a considerable number of women were enabled to take part in the referendum on 26 January 1963. Their votes were counted, and the results were published.[2]

The enthusiasm and the devotion to the Sháhansháh shown by the women on that day were truly unique in Iranian history. Not only teachers and the like, but also nomadic tribeswomen, cast favorable votes with tears of joy in their eyes. This spontaneous and earnest upsurge definitely expedited the enactment of legislation to grant Iranian women full civic and political rights as part of the Charter of the White Revolution of Shah and People.

A DEMONSTRATION OUTSIDE THE SENATE

A few days after the referendum, representatives of the women's associations marched through the streets of Tehran carrying banners which proclaimed their demand for women's suffrage in all elections. They went to the senate and, after demonstrating, were received by the president of the senate, who undertook to transmit to H.I.M. the Sháhansháh their petitions concerning women's readiness to serve in national and local elective bodies.

WOMEN'S GRATITUDE AND LOYALTY TO THE SHÁHANSHÁH

It was not long afterward that H.I.M. the Sháhansháh was due to inaugurate the Sháhnáz dam near Hamadán. On learning of this, certain representatives of the women's associations[3] were able, through the helpful efforts of a public-spirited lady, Mrs. Ferangis Yegánegi, to fly to Hamadán and arrive at the site while the ceremony was in progress. They took the opportunity to express to H.I.M. Sháhansháh in person their disgust at the disorders, aimed against women's freedom and staged by self-seeking wirepullers and reactionary agitators, which had taken place a few days before in the Tehran bazaar and had involved numbers of simple-minded and excitable people. The representatives affirmed the willingness and readiness of Iranian women for every sort of sacrifice on the path to achievement of their beloved sovereign's lofty aims. H.I.M. the Sháhansháh questioned the representatives very sympathetically about the relevant problems.

THE CHARTER OF EQUAL CITIZENSHIP

In the event, on the happily memorable day of 27 February 1963,[4] Iranian women were removed from the category of wards and minors and recognized as adults possessing all the rights and duties of Iranian citizenship equally with men.

It was on this day that the Charter of the White Revolution of Shah and People, with its recognition of women's full citizenship as an essential component of the revolution, was announced and published.

The announcement was made by H.I.M. the Sháhansháh in his opening speech at an economic conference. In the course of the speech he unexpectedly gave the good news when he said: "God willing, we shall remove this last blemish of Iranian society at the next elections, and all the citizens of this kingdom will then share in the voting for the parliament of Iran and in the shaping of their own future."

On 2 March 1963, the minister of the interior reported to the cabinet that a study of the Supplementary Fundamental Law of 30 September 1907 showed that it clearly states and lays down that "every citizen is entitled to share in the approval and supervision of public business." Moreover, according to article two of the Fundamental Law of 30 December 1906, "the National Consultative Assembly represents the whole of the people of the kingdom of Iran, who shall enjoy participation in the political and economic affairs of their homeland." On this basis, the report went on, no justification exists for the continued denial of voting rights to women. The cabinet accordingly revoked article ten, clause one, and article thirteen, clause two, of the parliamentary elections law of November 1911, which relate to qualifications of electors and candidates for election to the Majles; deleted the restrictive word male from articles six and nine of the senate elections law of 4 May 1949: and requested the minister of the interior to obtain legal validation of these measures from the two houses of parliament after their opening.

In another speech given after the publication of the charter, H.I.M. the Sháhansháh said:

> Thanks be to God that the last blemish on our society has now been removed, and the heavy chain of contempt and subjection which lay on the neck of half this country's people has been unfastened and smashed. In a country where young people of both sexes go side by side to primary school and secondary school and university, how can anyone dare to tell a woman who has passed all these stages that she is disqualified like a minor or a lunatic?

WOMEN IN PARLIAMENT AND IN ELECTED COUNCILS

Having acquired civic rights, Iranian women intended to make use of them. In particular, they would take part in the forthcoming parliamentary elections and would not be deterred by any adverse influences. This was made plain when they demonstrated in Tehran on 13 August 1963. At a meeting in the Bahárestán Square (opposite the Majles), they approved a manifesto expressing the readiness of Iranian women to take part in the elections and give effect to the charter of Iran's White Revolution.

The elections, in which a new Majles and half the membership of a new senate were chosen, took place on 17 September 1963. For the first time, women not only voted but also stood as candidates. Six were elected to the Majles and became Iran's first women deputies. At the same time Iran's first women senators were appointed; they were Dr. Shams ol-Moluk Mosáheb and Dr. Mehrangiz Menuchehrián, each of whom had been in the first group of twelve women students admitted to Tehran University in 1936. Thus the barrier which for decades had excluded Iranian women from the legislative process, and had allowed the passage of laws which took no account of them, was now broken.

The first woman to be elected to the senate—in 1971—was Mrs. Hájar Tarbiat, who had been the president of the Ladies' Center in 1935-1937.

Iranian women have begun to play their part in the field of local government, particularly since the new legislation of 1968 and 1970 concerning elected municipal, provincial and district councils. They have been elected to these councils and to mayoral positions. This is a field of community service in which women can contribute much.

A NEW CAMPAIGN AGAINST WOMEN'S ILLITERACY

After the proclamation of the equality of men's and women's rights and the subsequent celebrations and rejoicings, attention was again turned to the great obstacle lying in the path of Iranian women's progress. The majority of the nation's women had been trammeled by their upbringing with outworn ideas and notions; they had been trained, as the saying goes, "to enter the husband's house in a veil and leave it in a winding sheet." Feelings of inadequacy and servility had thereby been thoroughly inculcated into them. Now it was necessary to inform them of the rights which they had acquired and of the duties which would henceforth fall on them, and generally to prepare them for enjoyment of freedom and recognition of its limits.

Since women were prisoners of illiteracy and ignorance to a much greater extent than men, H.I.H. Princess Ashraf Pahlavi, as honorary president of the High Council of Iranian Women's Associations and a strong supporter of their work, called upon these associations to act without delay in organizing anti-illiteracy classes throughout the country. To acquaint the women with their new responsibilities, the candle of knowledge must be lit in every corner.

This royal initiative was welcomed with enthusiasm. The various associations all declared their readiness to join in this sacred duty and quickly got down to work.

THE FUTURE OF THE WOMEN'S MOVEMENT

In the course of a speech in February 1966 marking the third anniversary of the charter of equal rights, H.I.H. Princess Ashraf Pahlavi said:

> Those who expect to secure the objectives of the charter of 27 February by merely celebrating and speechifying, or by creating empty titles and superfluous organizations, either misunderstand the Sháhansháh's wishes, or knowingly or unknowingly betray the ideals of the revolution which has taken place in our country. For us, the ideals of this revolution will only be realized when our women's associations can mobilize the creative energies of the entirety of the country's women for the upbuilding of a free and prosperous community; and this historic mission can only be fulfilled by organizations which belong to the entire nation. The charter of 27 February makes it imperative that we go out to the mass of the people and study their deep-felt needs and pains ...

THE FAMILY PROTECTION LAW

While the charter of 27 February 1963 gave women equal rights as Iranian citizens, the Civil Code still denied them equal rights as spouses and parents. This was a matter of great concern to the women's associations, who pressed for reform and devoted much study and thought to the problems.

In the successive phases of human history, marriage has been regarded as a sacred and honorable contract. All religions have ordained special marriage laws, and every community or nation practices vivid and august ceremonies to emphasize its importance. In some religions, the union of husband and wife is indissoluble; and, in general, dissolution of this bond is reprehended because it breaks up the home and damages the well-being of the children, leaving them without the benefit of necessary care and supervision

The Winning of Equal Rights

by both parents. When the father and mother pull different ways and quarrel, children's delicate nerves are frayed and their natural development is impeded. Such ill-effects have wider harmful repercussions on the whole of society, which is made up of individuals from families.

In Iran, the former seclusion and subjection of women left this vital matter wholly at the whim of men. The wife in her husband's home had no wage, no insurance, no holiday entitlements, no pension rights, and was in reality just an unpaid or capriciously paid servant, with the difference that the husband could unexpectedly divorce and evict her at any moment he chose —in which case she would not, if she was a mother, have any right to the custody of her own beloved children or even a right to information about their health and activities.

This state of affairs had come into being in spite of the fact that the holy religion of Islam has never permitted such unjust and irresponsible conduct by men. On the contrary, Islam endows women with full human rights and privileges and grants them independent economic personality; it strictly limits polygamy, requires the father to maintain his children, and enjoins good and equitable treatment of the wife.

There is no doubt that the frequent violation of family rights by Iranian men made Iranian women feel so insecure that they lived in constant anxiety. They could not regard the home, the children, the family belongings, as their own. They felt as if they were lodgers, temporarily staying in a house but having no attachment to it or interest in it.

The Family Protection Law of 1967 went far to meet the long-standing hopes and demands of the women's associations for reform of this state of affairs. The bill, which was drafted at the wish of H.I.M. the Sháhansháh and submitted by the Ministry of Justice to the two houses of parliament in February 1967, received their approval and became law on 15 July 1967.

This law will clearly aid not only women's and children's welfare, but also men's peace of mind and happiness. In former times, it often happened that a boy from an insecure home or broken family fled in despair and then for the rest of his life bore bitter grudges against his parents and the whole human race; or that a man broke up his family in a moment of folly or temptation and then lived in undying remorse for the grim consequences of his deed; or that he irresponsibly embarked on polygamy and then endured the agonies of financial distress and discord between conflicting spouses and their offspring.

Since the enactment of the Family Protection Law, whose provisions wholly conform with the God-given precepts of Islam, husbands can no longer arbitrarily and without good cause repudiate their wives. A decree of divorce can only be granted after investigation of the case and issue of a certificate of irreconcilability by a court of law. Another provision lays down that a married man cannot take an additional wife at his own pleasure, but is required to prove that he has valid grounds for so doing and sufficient means to maintain two families. Can he ever truly give such proof? In any case, if he takes a second wife, the first wife can now demand divorce.

Under this law, the court has jurisdiction in the matter of children's maintenance. It entrusts the custody of the children to whichever parent or third party can best ensure their well-being and education, and makes the expense of their upbringing a charge on the income of either parent or both. Divorce cannot be effected until the position of the children has been settled.

The Family Protection Law contains provisions for divorce on the initiative of the wife, which hitherto had not normally been possible, and these are of value in certain situations.

Of course, there are imperfections in the Family Protection Law, and there have been difficulties in its implementation, and there are also fields where reform is needed but on which it does not touch. Even so, it will undoubtedly be of great importance for the future security of wives and well-being of families, subject to one condition. This is that the mental backgrounds and consciences of young people must be prepared through appropriate instruction and education for acceptance of the principle of equality of human rights. They must be helped to understand the evils which spring from unjust and offensive behavior and to make equitable dealing their unwritten law. In parallel with this, girls must be instilled with a sense of duty and a knowledge of the greater responsibilities which now fall on them in a more advanced society. Legislation does not of itself change people's minds; it bears fruit when it is matched by a nation's educational and moral advancement.

A TRIUMPH FOR IRANIAN WOMEN

In the same year as the passage of the Family Protection Law, another great success shiningly exemplified the rise in status of Iranian wives and mothers. This was the designation of H.I.M. the Empress Farah as prospective regent by a constituent assembly in May 1967, and her coronation by the nation's courageous leader, her royal husband, on 26 October 1967.

Iranian men and women are well aware that this success sprang mainly from the high moral character, and the understanding and humanity and philanthropy, of which H.I.M. the Empress has given abundant proof. While worthily performing her duties as an affectionate and dignified consort and as a caring and strict mother, she has at the same time toiled unremittingly to give practical effect to H.I.M. the Sháhansháh's aim of uplifting Iranian society and enabling all classes to enjoy a better and more cultured and more healthy life. She has shown a particular concern for youth problems and youth guidance.

The law, since the constitutional amendment of 1967, is that only a man may be shah, but a woman may be regent and temporarily perform the shah's functions.

THE WOMEN'S LITERACY CORPS

In accordance with the sixth point of the White Revolution, young men holding the diploma of secondary education are given an option to serve in the Literacy Corps instead of doing the usual two years of military service. Members of this corps, which was instituted in 1963, are sent to teach literacy in the villages and are encouraged to do all in their power to eradicate general ignorance. The Health Corps, set up in 1964, and the Development and Extension Corps, set up in 1965, similarly provide medical, agricultural, and developmental help to the hitherto deprived rural areas. The zeal and achievements of these social service corps since they started work have earned worldwide admiration.

Meanwhile, and also as a result of the White Revolution, women had ceased to be unprivileged servants of men and were enjoying equal status with men in human rights and dignity. It was essential that young women should acknowledge the principle of equal responsibility also and that, while enjoying rightful freedoms, they should prove their worth in the performance of needed services for the country. One of the main duties of a nation's educated elements is to hasten to the aid of backward and needy groups and thereby help to develop the intellectual and functional capacity of the whole community.

In the light of these considerations, the Women's Literacy Corps was finally established in 1968. Besides enabling women to join with men in this estimable form of national service, it has other merits. The well-educated girls serving in it enter easily into contact and understanding with women living in isolated villages or urban slums who have had no chance to get any schooling and are quite ignorant of family management and hygiene. Having thus come to grips with problems of their fellow citizens, the girls acquire eagerness and competence to do further social service or charitable work.

Another merit of this corps is that it bridges the gap between different classes in a town, or between townfolk and countryfolk, resulting from imbalances in the rate of change of each. New phenomena are spreading uniformly throughout the country and enabling all its inhabitants to mix and become acquainted. With better understanding, the men and women of the villages will no longer envy and resent the city dwellers, and the dwellers in mean sections of the cities will lose their bitterness against the dwellers in better sections. Conversely, the well-off women will cease to feel and show disdain for the backward.

The Women's Literacy Corps also promotes better understanding between young women and young men. When both possess shared experience of corps service and social work, and shared memories of the system and the discipline, they develop similar ways of thinking and styles of living. In the joint enterprise of running a household and raising a family, this harmony of thought and conduct can be a great help to them.

Thus the Women's Literacy Corps, though formed for the specific purpose of disseminating literacy and sound practices of hygiene, housekeeping and child-rearing among backward families in remote villages and depressed sections of cities, brings concurrent advantages of great importance to the women who serve in it.

The women of today form the connecting link between past and future generations. They have turned their backs on a dark past and are stepping forth to a bright future. It is their duty to see what is needed, and give what is needed, for the rise of a sturdy young generation in every corner of Iran.

NEW HORIZONS OF WORK AND SERVICE

The White Revolution removed legal barriers against women's employment and, by influencing public opinion, has helped to remove social barriers.

Cabinet office was first given to a woman in 1968, when Dr. Farrokhru Pársá became minister of education.[5] In the civil service women have risen to high ranks such as director general and head of department.

In all three armed forces, women serve side by side with men and have won distinction. They have been commissioned as officers in the army, air force, and navy.

The ranks of the police are also open to women, who have shown eagerness to enlist and aptitude for the work. Many serve in traffic departments.

Women law graduates of Iranian universities were entitled to practice as advocates and solicitors equally with men, but could not become judges until after the White Revolution. The first woman law graduate and practicing lawyer was Dr. Mehrangiz Menuchehrián.[6]

Women have a special skill in settling disputes. Whenever

sympathy can help, they are better than men at tactfully disposing of acrimonious quarrels, at changing anger and contention into calm and peace.

When houses of equity were established in rural areas in 1963 and arbitration councils in urban areas in 1966 for the speedy adjudication of minor cases, women were made eligible for election to these bodies so that they might share in finding verdicts and passing sentences on men and women alike.

In 1968 a number of girl students of the law faculty of Tehran University were inducted into a practical training course at the Tehran Public Prosecutions Office. After graduating and gaining further experience in the courts, they were raised to the bench as the country's first women judges. Another disability long endured by Iranian women thus came to an end.

The first Iranian women physicians and surgeons rendered immense services, particularly to their fellow women, when they started work after graduating from the Tehran faculty of medicine or from medical colleges abroad. They saved the lives of many women whose ignorant and prejudice-ridden families would not allow a male doctor to examine or operate on a sick woman. This prejudice, and the similar prejudice which inhibited families from allowing their daughters to become hospital nurses, have now almost wholly disappeared. The number of women doctors has grown steadily, though it is still too small for the country's needs. In Iranian hospitals thousands of trained nurses are now devotedly caring for male and female patients. Since 1968 women have been serving in the Health Corps and have shown a special ability to help and guide the families of villagers. Several new medical faculties and nursing schools have been established, and girl students have eagerly enrolled in them.

The growth in women's employment as secretaries has been particularly striking. The ministries and offices and banks of present-day Iran could not function without their help. Employment of women in shops has also increased, though relatively at a lesser rate.

Teaching is still the profession which educated women eager

The Winning of Equal Rights

to serve the community prefer. They serve in every rank, from primary-school teacher to university professor.

As scholars, writers, artists, film actresses, dress designers, and in other fields, Iranian women have won laurels at home and abroad. The efforts of the Iranian women's movement also have received international appreciation.

INTERNATIONAL APPRECIATION OF THE IRANIAN WOMEN'S MOVEMENT

Since the winning of equal rights for men and women in 1963, representatives of the world's women have expressed appreciation of the efforts of the Iranian women's movement and admiration for the bold step taken by H.I.M. the Sháhansháh. Only the most important of these international women's gatherings can be mentioned here, as a discussion of them all would exceed the limits of this short book.

On 20 April 1963, the International Conference of Women met in Tehran. H.I.H. Princess Ashraf Pahlavi opened its proceedings, at which problems affecting women throughout the world were reviewed.

In June 1963, the International Council of Women at its conference in Washington showed its gratitude for H.I.M. the Sháhansháh's action by calling upon H.I.H. Princess Ashraf Pahlavi to speak first.

At the World Congress of Women in Moscow, which was opened on 24 June 1963, great admiration for the successes of Iranian women was expressed.

The International Commission on the Status of Women held its fourteenth session—its first in an Asian country—at the Hilton Hotel in Tehran in March 1965. The opening ceremony on 1 March was performed by H.I.M. the Empress Farah. Iran had been chosen as the venue in recognition of the importance of H.I.M. the Sháhansháh's initiative for equality of women's rights. On the same day H.I.H. Princess Ashraf was elected president of the session.

The International Council of Women met in Tehran again in May 1966. The conference was opened on 16 May 1966 by H.I.M. the Empress Farah, who said in her speech of welcome: "By virtue of this gathering, our city symbolizes the continuing great fight of women all over the world to achieve their supreme goal, namely the practical implementation of the equality which the Declaration of Human Rights has officially proclaimed."

The first international Conference on Human Rights was held in Tehran and opened on 23 April 1968 by H.I.M. the Sháhansháh, who made an important speech. H.I.H. Princess Ashraf Pahlavi was elected president of the conference in recognition of her assiduous efforts to raise the status of women. The discussions centered on progress made in the previous twenty years toward enforcement of the Universal Declaration of Human Rights. The conference published resolutions concerning steps which it thought necessary for the international advancement of human rights, and completed its proceedings in a stirring session on 13 May, when the delegates from the eighty-one member countries passed the Tehran Declaration.

The most important inference to be drawn from these occasions is that Iran has not only pulled itself out of an unhappy phase by means of a real revolution, but has now taken the lead in work to implant justice and peace in the world. This is clearly proved by the choice of Tehran for such gatherings.

Observers of the rapid changes in Iran's social and economic condition and political standing, which in a short period have brought the country from a dark past into a bright present, feel that there are good grounds to admire the achievements of Iranian men and women and to thank God for giving them such wise leadership.

THE TASK AHEAD

The charter of equality given by the Sháhansháh on 27 February 1963 removed Iranian women from the category of wards and minors and recognized them as adults possessing full human rights. Since that date they have borne the heavy responsibilities of full citizenship with complete awareness and faith. They know that they have the duty of rearing the future citizens of a nation whose thinkers and statesmen and heroes have bequeathed teachings and counsels, and examples of good conduct, which were and are of benefit to the world. The Iranians, when they degraded their women and lost respect for their mothers, had copied deceptive, external aspects of other scenes and fallen into error. If the Iranian women of today use reason and common sense in combining their spiritual heritage from the past with the realities of modern knowledge, they can hope to succeed in the task of guiding the next generation to happiness.

NOTES

1. 6 Bahman 1341 in the Iranian calendar.
2. Translator's note: 5,598,000 men voted yes, 415,000 men voted no, 271,000 women voted unofficially yes.
3. Translator's note: including the authoress.
4. 8 Esfand 1341 in the Iranian calendar.
5. See p. 76.
6. See p. 102.

APPENDIX A

SOME POEMS

In a book which compares the happy fate of the young, emancipated Iranian women of today with the bitter sufferings of their mothers in the not-so-distant past, and which records the efforts of pioneers who struggled in an environment of ignorance and fanaticism to change the former deplorable status of Iranian women, it would not be fitting to omit a mention of the now-famous poets and poetesses who fearlessly cried out against the repression and waste of women's talents and the evils of veiling and seclusion. Despite all the unfavorable influences, the beauty and sincerity of their words carried their message to the ears of the people. Some of their poems were soon known by heart and sung or recited in the streets and bazaars. These poems had a powerful effect in correcting mistaken notions and guiding to better ways.

The bravest and most celebrated of them were the poetess Parvin E'tesámi (1906-1941), and the poets Áref Qazvini (c. 1882-1934), Hájj Mirzá Yahyá Dowlatábádi (1862-1939), Malek ol-Sho'ará Bahár (1886-1950), Iraj Mirzá Jalál ol-Mamálek (1874-1925), and Mirzázádeh Eshqi (1893-1924). Translations of some moving and well-known poems by five of them[1] appear in this appendix.

Parvin E'tesámi was a woman of noble character and great poetic talent. She has a high place in Persian literature. Her sensitive nature enabled her to overcome the barriers which separated her (like other women at that time) from the rest of society. She succeeded in sensing the pains, injustices, and hardships endured by the mass of the people and in casting them into a mold of charming and moving verse. Her collected poems are so highly appreciated that every new edition which is published soon goes out of print. The poem quoted below is one of the greatest literary masterpieces in the Persian language. Written in March 1936, a few weeks after the unveiling, it perfectly expresses the feelings of Iranian women at that time.

"WOMEN IN IRAN," PARVIN E'TESÁMI (1906-1941)

Until this day, women in Iran could not be called Iranians,
because for them ways to serve were barred;
only anguish and grief lay open.

They lived and died apart, in the corner of solitude;
truly they were no more than prisoners, in those now bygone days.
Only the women dwelt in darkness for centuries;
they alone were sacrificed on the altar of hypocrisy.
Only the women had no advocate in the court of equity;
they alone had no schooling in the academy of merit.
The women's pleas for justice remained unheard in their lifetimes,
and the injustice was not hidden, but overt.
There were folk who wore smocks and carried crooks,
but at heart were just wolves in shepherd's attire.
In life's broad field the women were condemned to narrowness.
The women were not inferior or stupid, but were ignorant,
because the light of knowledge was kept hidden from women's eyes.
Crops are not won unless the farmer has tools and training;
so how could the women weave without spindle, thread or skill?
Much was offered on the fruit stall of knowledge,
but never any share to the women.

Forced to live in a cage and to die in a cage,
these garden birds were not seen or heard in the garden.
Their road led through wastes of anxiety to wells of woe;
only clever ones could break away from this grim road.
The adornment which makes a complexion truly fair is knowledge;
emeralds and Badakhshán rubies were no proof of merit.

Gold and jewels make no difference when the women lack knowledge;
such things cannot conceal the blemish of ignorance.

Women are guardians; virtue is their treasure, lust or greed is the thief,
and disaster comes if they are not vigilant.
The eye and the heart need a veil, but one of self-discipline;
the frail cloak of cloth was not a bulwark of Moslem faith.

"WOMEN IN SHROUDS," MIRZÁZÁDEH ESHQI (1893-1924)

You are hot-blooded, Eshqi, your heart quickly melts!
If girls lifted the veil, you would see their cheeks!
Well, this poem is about veiling, though wholly against it.
Uncountable evils have sprung from the veil.
The task of a poet is to give counsel to others.
So speak freely and speak without fear!

Why the fuss? Men are God's servants and women are too.
What have women done wrong to feel shame before men?
What are these unbecoming, uncouth, cloaks and veils?
They are winding sheets meant for the dead, not the living.
I say, "Death to the men who bury women alive
in the name of religion!" That is enough to say here.

If two or three poets add their voices to mine,
the people will soon start humming this song.
Their hums will uncover the women's fair faces,
the women will proudly throw off their vile masks,
the people will then have some joy in their lives.
But, otherwise, what will become of Iran?
With the women in shrouds, half the nation is dead.

"NO MORE VEILS LIKE THESE,"
MALEK OL-SHO'ARÁ BAHÁR (1886-1950)

To hold a husband's heart, a wife
  needs more than charm alone.

A moonlike fairy face may go
  together with a shrewish tongue.

A plainer face may signify
a deeper love, a truer grace.

Men are prosaic, women are
poetic. God has made them so.

Man, woman and Creator are
each different in kind. When joined
to one another, they produce
a winning combination.[2]

Morality is not insured
by veils and covers, which indeed
encourage taking liberties.

Bahár wants no more veils like these!

"Ruffled Locks," Áref Qazvini (1882-1934)

Lift the veil from your beautiful, moonlike face!
Pay no heed to the impudent preacher's rude words!
Lift the veil with your delicate, silver-hued hands!
Never mind if the blame for it falls on my head!
Ruffle the prigs with your lovely ruffled tresses and locks!
And ignore their vain threats without turning a hair!

"The Hypocrisy of the Veil," Iraj Mirzá Jalál ol-Mamálek (Son of Sadr ol-Sho'ará; 1874-1925)

They wear veils, those whose beauty fascinates us.
Unless that beauty's veiled, we're told, God help us!
Our city's preachers are against unveiling,
because they like to veil their own deceptions.
When God's words in the Qor'án do not suit them,
they find false explanations, hidden meanings.
I once was asked to solve a knotty problem
and could not: why among all living creatures,
Iranians alone choose unseen partners?
When will a group of our veiled women muster
the manly courage to reject their face masks?

Appendix A

>It is the veil which makes this bunch of clerics
>the masters of one-half of all our nation.
>If I speak to your wife, you need not worry;
>but if your wife speaks to your sister, watch out!
>On pilgrimage at Mecca women walk round
>the Ka'ba with no veils; so tell these preachers,
>to rush to Mecca and demolish God's house!
>We shall not lift the veil through moderation.
>We need a helping hand from revolution
>to tear apart these gloomy clouds of darkness
>and fill our streets with sunlight and with moonlight.

NOTES

1. It has been necessary to omit a poem by Yahyá Dowlatábádi entitled "Women's Dignity" (*Maqám-e Zan*) because of translation difficulties.
2. The poet refers to a position in the game of backgammon.

APPENDIX B

PUBLICATIONS EDITED BY WOMEN (1909-1969)

1. *Dánesh (Knowledge)*, periodical. There is evidence that a magazine of this name was published in or about 1909 by the wife of Dr. Hoseyn Khán Kahhál.
2. *Shokufeh (Blossom)*, newspaper. Published in 1912, edited by Mozayyen ol-Saltaneh, daughter of Mirzá Seyyed Razi Rayis ol-Atebbá.
3. *Zabán-e Zanán (Women's Voice)*, periodical. Published at Esfahán in 1920, edited by Sadiqeh Dowlatábádi.
4. *Jahán-e Zanán (Women's World)*, periodical. Published first at Mashhad and then at Tehran, edited by Fakhr-e Áfáq Pársá. Banned after a few issues.
5. *Majalle-ye Nesván-e Vatankhwáh (Patriotic Women's Magazine)*, periodical. Published in 1923, edited by Moluk Eskandari. Organ of the Patriotic Women's League.
6. *Álam-e Nesván (Women's Universe)*, periodical. First published in 1920, when Navvábeh Safavi was editor and Miss Boyce manager. Lasted until 1935. Periodical of the graduates of the American Girls' School.
7. *Peyk-e Sa'ádat (Courier of Happiness)*, periodical. Published at Rasht in 1925, edited by Rowshanak Now'dust.
8. *Dokhtarán-e Irán (Daughters of Iran)*, periodical. Published at Shiráz, 1931-32, edited by Zand-dokht Shirázi.
9. *Zan-e Emruz (Women Today)*, periodical. Published 1944-1955, edited by Badr ol-Moluk Bámdád.
10. *Rahnomá-ye Zendegi (Guide to Living)*, periodical. Published in 1941, edited by Máh-Tal'at Pesián.

11. *Rastákhiz-e Irán (Renaissance of Iran)*, daily newspaper. Published in 1942, edited by Irán Teymurtásh.
12. *Majalle-ye Bánu (Ladies Magazine)*, periodical. Published in 1944, edited by Neyyer Sa'idi.
13. *Hoquq-e Zanán (Women's Rights)*, newspaper. Published in 1945, edited by Ebteháj Mostaheqqi.
14. *Bibi (Housewife)*, periodical. Published in 1945, edited by Nur ol-Hodá Manganeh.
15. *Sapide-ye Fardá (Dawn of Tomorrow)*. Published by the Faculty of Education of Tehran University since 1952, edited by Ázar Rahnomá.
16. *Ettelá'at-e Bánuván (Ladies News)*. Magazine affiliated with Ettelá'át newspaper, edited by Qodsi Mas'udi.
17. *Zan-e Ruz (The Modern Woman)*. Magazine affiliated with Keyhán newspaper, edited by Forugh Mesbáhzádeh.
18. *Post-e Irán (Iranian Post)*, periodical. Published independently since 1963 by A'zam Sepehr-Khádem, president of the Women's Awakening Society.